A Modern Trapline

A Modern Trapline

Methods & Materials

Bob Gilsvik

Illustrations by David Gilsvik

Chilton Book Company   Radnor, Pennsylvania

Library of Congress Cataloging in Publication Data

Gilsvik, Bob.
    A modern trapline.

    1. Trapping   I. Title.
SK283.G47 1980   639'.11   78-14650
ISBN 0-0819-6781-3

Designed by Arlene Putterman
Manufactured in the United States of America
All photographs are by Bob or David Gilsvik except as noted.
All names of manufacturers and products should be
considered registered trademarks.

**To Charlie Mechley
for his generous answers
to my seemingly endless questions**

Contents

Preface

Running a fulltime trapline as the final "research" for this book was, for me, a fantasy come true. An enthusiastic hunter and fisherman, I've also been a part-time trapper for 30 years. But the trapline my son Dave and I ran in the winter of 1978–79 was our first *fulltime* trapline—and what an adventure that was! Moreover, this kind of adventure is open to anyone, and you do not have to live on some tributary of the Yukon River or in a cabin in Alaska to realize it. Our trapline was operated from our home in a small town in north central Minnesota. We could have done as well, if not better, in Pennsylvania, Maine, or Missouri. The Louisiana trapper would surely have bested us in trapping muskrat, and I know that they have a lot more raccoon in Ohio. The fact is, there are few places in North America where one cannot pursue the pleasure, and the profits, of running a trapline.

A segment of our society believes trapping is unnecessary. Mother Nature, they say, can take care of her own. Experienced game management professionals and wildlife biologists strongly disagree. With civilization's continual encroachment upon once-wild lands, controlling wildlife populations has become a serious problem. Nature's "cure" for a surplus in a confined area is malnutrition and disease. While hunting is the best method of controlling populations of deer and other large animals, it is extremely inefficient for controlling that of the smaller animals. Professional wildife biologists agree that well-managed traplines are the most effective tools available for this purpose.

A MODERN TRAPLINE

Many people do not realize that there are seasonal limits to trapping. Trapping is restricted by law to a few months in fall and winter. The current season on otter in Minnesota is only two weeks long. By setting the length of the various seasons, by setting the season limits, and by occasionally banning trapping of certain species, the game department can keep furbearer numbers at a healthy level.

Most states have a complicated set of trapping laws. In Minnesota last year, there was a limit of six bobcat, three fisher, and three otter per trapper. These animals had to be tagged at the site where caught and turned into the nearest game department for additional tagging and registration. Because muskrat numbers were low from drought conditions a few years previous, trapping in muskrat houses was prohibited. On the other hand, because beaver numbers were extremely high, a longer season was allowed to bring their numbers under control. In fact, of the popular animals trapped for their fur in the United States—muskrat, mink, skunk, raccoon, fox, and beaver—all were reported as being overabundant in one area or another in a 1974 survey of fish and wildlife commissioners.

State laws will also govern what kind of traps may be used and where, and how often your traps must be checked. Snaring, for example, is illegal in some states. In Minnesota, the entire trapline must be checked at least once every 36 hours.

Are traps really so painful? An animal's foot quickly grows numb when caught in a trap. Most land animals such as fox, coyote, and raccoon are caught by the toes or across the pad of the foot. These animals have such fast reflexes that they may frequently lift a foot fast enough to escape the closing of the trap. But when caught, a trapped animal may feel some pain for a short time in a leg-hold trap until its foot becomes numb. Then after an initial struggle to free itself, it will usually curl up and sleep soundly. A trapped fox or raccoon may often be closely approached before it awakens.

In many states there is pressure to outlaw the leg-hold trap in favor of the Conibear® or killer trap. While there are many advantages to the killer trap, particularly in water sets for mink, muskrat, and beaver, they cannot replace the leg-hold trap. The leg-hold trap is designed to catch animals alive, restrain them, and leave the decision to free or retain the captured animal to the trapper. They are an invaluable tool of wildlife research. Natural history studies frequently involve the trapping of individual animals so they can be examined, aged, sexed, weighed, tagged, and then released unharmed. Retrapping these same animals later provides invaluable information on their movements and condition.

PREFACE

In writing my earlier book, *The Complete Book of Trapping,* I drew upon the expertise of many other trappers because my own experience had been limited to the trapping of mink, muskrat, and other short-furred animals whose pelts have been so popular. But now the prices for long-furred animals have soared, and even the short-furred animals continue to bring acceptable prices. I and my son Dave, who collaborated with me and did the illustrations for this book and others, were eager to gain firsthand, fulltime experience trapping a great variety of animals.

The reader can benefit not only from what we did right in our trapping, but also from what we did wrong. And we made mistakes. I learned that planning for all the little things that go into a fulltime trapline gets complicated. We hope you can use what we learned in planning your own trapline, whether it's for a full season, a week's vacation, or a weekend.

A
Modern
Trapline

1
The Animals and Their Characteristics

Over a four-month period, from mid-October thru mid-February, we trapped nine species of animals, including fox, raccoon, mink, muskrat, coyote, bobcat, fisher, beaver, and otter. We trapped beaver again for a short period in April. While the emphasis of this book is to describe the methods and convey the adventure of running a modern trapline, a preliminary discussion of the animals and their characteristics should be helpful.

Fox

The red fox is about three feet long, including a tail of about one foot. The underside of its reddish-brown coat is whiter in color, and the back of its ears and its lower legs are black. The largest I've seen weighed 16 pounds, but 9 to 12 pounds is average.

Extensive studies of the red fox and its prey in many parts of the world, including natural fox populations in Britain, Sweden, and the United States and introduced populations in Australia, have shown that this predator concentrates mainly on small rodents, rabbits, and hares.

But a picture also emerges of a versatile hunter that will eat, if the opportunity presents itself, carrion, ground-nesting birds and their young,

1

Figure 1-1 Prime red foxes like this one are in great demand and bring top prices.

bird's eggs, fruit, sheep placentas in the lambing season, beetles, and, increasingly in cities, the contents of garbage cans.

Good eyesight, acute hearing, an excellent sense of smell, plus a timid and suspicious nature make the fox one of the most difficult of all animals to trap. It's not only afraid of human beings, but also is equally afraid of a stranger of its own kind. For this reason we would always place a trap in an open area instead of heavy, brushy surroundings. A fox will come in "on his nose" and, as he approaches the set (the trap and its camouflage), he will be assured by complete vision of the surrounding area that all is clear and there is nothing to fear. A fox, particularly a young red, does not like to approach a set in heavy cover simply because he has no assurance that the "fox" he smells has left the area. Only when he can be completely satisfied that no other fox or human is nearby will he investigate the set.

Red foxes are afraid of the greys, but most grey foxes are not afraid of the reds; therefore, it is always advisable to use red fox urine in making a set if you are trapping in an area where both species are present.

Both species of foxes will shy from anything foreign, whether it be sound, sight, or odor. A crackling piece of wax paper used as a trap pan cover will frighten a fox. (Be sure to use wax paper that has been crumpled, unrolled, and recrumpled several times.) A partially exposed, shiny steel trap is not a natural object in the forest and will call a halt to a fox's investigation of your set just as readily as human or other unnatural odors will.

While red foxes can be found almost anywhere, they prefer open farm lands. We have no grey foxes on our trapline. The grey fox shows a preference for heavier undergrowth, such as briar thickets, scrub oaks, huckleberry, laurel, and rhododendron swamps.

Raccoon

Raccoon vary in size and weight depending on age and the available food supply. Some will reach a total body length, including the tail, of 40 inches and weigh over 35 pounds, while the average is 15 to 20 pounds. I heard of one caught in our area that weighed 45 pounds. Raccoon are grizzled grey in color and have a "bandit's" mask and a thick bushy tail with alternating rings of yellowish-white and black.

The raccoon is an omnivorous feeder. It likes fish, frogs, shellfish, small mammals, birds and bird eggs, reptiles, insects, fruit, corn, and is not adverse to rummaging in garbage dumps. Around the farm, it will kill poultry, steal eggs, and raid the dog's food dish. It is not unusual to find raccoon on the very edge of, or even in, towns and cities. A family of raccoon can completely wreck a gardener's patch of sweet corn in one night.

Because raccoon are not timid or suspicious, they are not a difficult animal to trap. Big, robust, and well-furred, the raccoon is a powerful animal and terrific scrapper. The biggest problem in trapping raccoon is holding one in the trap once it is caught.

Raccoon can be found almost anywhere in farming country and forest, but there is usually a stream, swamp, or lake within the mile or so diameter of the raccoon's territorial limit. Large rivers and streams are especially attractive to raccoon. My son Dave ran a boat trapline for raccoon and found it an interesting outdoor experience, since mink and muskrat were also found along the trapline and foxes in adjacent fields.

Mink

Mink have body lengths of 18 to 24 inches, including their 8 inch tails. We caught one that measured 35 inches from nose to tail tip on the drying board. It weighed over four pounds, while the average is one to three pounds. The body is dark brown, the tail almost black.

Like most members of the weasel family, the mink is a solitary wanderer. Generally found near water, the mink trails by scent, captures small game and birds, and varies its diet with fish, frogs, crustaceans, and other forms of aquatic life. The mink is adept at capturing and killing its prey. I once watched a mink spring from a creek bank and sink its teeth into the base of a muskrat's neck. They rolled over and over for 20 feet down the creek, and the muskrat was dead within seconds. The mink, obviously a large male, dragged it off into the underbrush.

The larger male mink are quite smart and therefore harder to trap. However, their inclination to travel much greater distances than the females increases the chances of their being caught in traps. Mink have a keen sense of smell and to catch one on dry land requires the same caution used in trapping fox. Catching mink with traps set in the water is easier since the trap, if it has been blackened, is almost invisible. A leg-hold trap placed under two inches of water will not give off a foreign odor that might warn a trap-wise mink.

We took further precautions at set locations by wearing hip boots and making all sets while standing in the water. We entered and exited a stream some distance up or downstream from set locations, and when a set was complete we splashed water over the stream bank and the whole set location to wash away any odors we might have left.

4

THE ANIMALS AND THEIR CHARACTERISTICS

Mink are found along lakes, rivers, creeks, water-filled ditches, and small brooks. After freeze-up, you'll find their tracks in the snow in swamps and marshes.

Muskrat

The average muskrat weighs two to five pounds and measures 18 to 25 inches including the tail, which is 8 to 11 inches, black, scaly, and flat-sided. Fur color is blackish on the back blending to brown and almost reddish tones on the side with a light, silvery belly. In north central Minnesota, muskrats are small, probably due to the lack of aquatic vegetation.

An insatiable eater, the muskrat modifies his diet according to available vegetation and will eat the roots and stems of a wide variety of plants, including cattail, bulrush, and lotus. It will also eat clams, snails, crayfish, and even other muskrats. It may eat its own house if built of tasty roots. Muskrat are frequently active both day and night.

Little knowledge is required to outsmart this prolific little rodent. Its tracks along the bank at the water's edge, its dung piles on a partly submerged log or on a stone protruding above the level of the water, the shredded grasses along the shoreline—all are proof of its presence. We had only to set our traps in places where this animal feeds and travels to catch it.

Look for them in swamps, marshes, lakes, rivers, creeks, and water-filled ditches. If there is water, you'll probably find muskrats.

Coyote

The coyote or "brush wolf" is uniformily grizzled grey in color, although some tend to be darker or lighter depending on the area in which they are caught. The lighter or paler colored coyote has commanded the highest pelt price in recent years. They will weigh from 20 to 50 pounds. Those we caught weighed between 25 and 30 pounds.

During the six winters from 1968 to 1974, researchers in northern Minnesota collected 1,305 coyote carcasses from furbuyers, trappers, and hunters. From these carcasses, 925 stomachs contained sufficient food for analysis. This tedious job, involving microscopic examination of animal hairs, resulted in interesting factual data on the coyote's diet. The five major food items found in stomachs were deer, mice, porcupine, livestock, and snowshoe hare.

But the stomach analysis only told what the coyote ate, not how it obtained that food. Subsequently, researchers followed 381 miles of winter coyote trails, often on snowshoes, to determine hunting and feeding activity. By this method it was learned that most deer fed on by coyotes were already dead, in carrion form. Coyotes, like many wild predators, are opportunists and may consume anything they believe edible.

Good eyesight, acute hearing, an excellent sense of smell—the coyote has it all, and then some. It is far more difficult to lure into a trap than either the fox or mink. As in trapping the red fox, sets for coyote must be made in open areas, although not open to the extent required for the more timid red fox.

While timber wolves exist today in wilderness areas away from man, coyotes are apt to be found in mixed habitats where forests and scattered farms intermingle.

Bobcat

The bobcat resembles a large tabby cat. An adult stands about 20 to 30 inches at the shoulder and weighs 10 to 40 pounds. The bobcat's body is longer than that of a domestic cat and its paws are more massive, with distinct five-sided heel pads. The biggest one we caught weighed 30 pounds, though it looked twice that size. Its coat is light fawn to rust brown, boldly streaked and spotted with black. Its common name is derived from its six-inch "bobtail," which is barred in black three or four times across the top and white underneath. The tip is white.

The bobcat feeds heavily on the snowshoe hare, though not to the same extent as the Canada lynx. Bobcats are also opportunists who will eat whatever is available. They often prey heavily on porcupine and, like the coyote, will dine on deer carrion.

Bobcat are not difficult to trap, but they are far-ranging animals in the winter months and their hunting routes are erratic. The problem, especially if the bobcats are few in number, is getting one to notice your bait. Their sense of smell is notoriously poor.

In northern forested areas, bobcat favor dense lowlands of spruce and balsam, as well as alder swamps that contain plenty of snowshoe rabbits and ruffed and spruce grouse.

Fisher

The fisher, although a member of the weasel family, is almost foxlike in appearance. Its length varies from 34 to 40 inches, including its 12 inch tail. The male may be twice the size of the female and weigh up to 20 pounds. Coloration is dark brown, almost black with a hint of grey. The fur of the female is much silkier than that of the male and pelts of prime females bring the best prices. We got up to $150 for a single pelt.

The fisher is the only animal that habitually dines on porcupines. Small game compose a fisher's diet, including rabbits, birds, and a variety of small rodents. Anything not eaten is buried for future use. The fisher will eat carrion or bury it for a later meal.

The fisher is not trap-wise. However, like the bobcat, it follows erratic hunting routes. If you can get one to see or smell your bait, you've got him. Fisher favor wild terrain. You've usually got to get away from the roads to find them. I've had the best luck in old cut-over areas, where the timber has been harvested and second growth is coming up.

Beaver

Overall length of beaver can reach four feet, and weight can approach the 70-pound mark, although the average weight is 30 to 40 pounds. The beaver's tail is broad, flat, and scaly. The guard hairs are a glistening chestnut brown, and the soft, luxurious underfur has a reddish tinge. The feet have five toes, and the hind feet are fully webbed.

The beaver's food consists of the bark, twigs, and even the wood of deciduous trees, with a marked preference for poplars, cottonwoods, willows, and alders. The poplar (aspen), found throughout the northern forested region of the United States and Canada, is probably the most sought after by beaver. In the western and prairie states, cottonwood is often the beaver's choice.

Where beavers have been trapped for a number of years the adults become very trap-wise and their cunning tests the skill of the real professional. Too much disturbance around the house during the trap-setting season will be ample warning for an adult to stay within the house for several weeks, living on the food brought into the house by the younger beavers.

More of the big adult beaver are taken during early winter or spring seasons when there is open water. This allows the traps to be set with much less disturbance and keeps the inexperienced trapper from tramping around the house. Open-water trapping for beavers is much like open-water trapping for muskrats, except that heavier traps and gear are used.

Beaver favor wooded terrain and create a pond or series of ponds from an insignificant trickle of water. It is not unusual for beaver to build a dam in a roadside ditch and to flood the road. Because beaver colonies can occur almost anywhere, in backwoods terrain or roadside ditch, trappers should make note of beaver signs—felled trees, dams, and lodges—whenever they are afield.

Otter

Overall body length for otter—which can include a heavy tail up to 18 inches in length—is 35 to 55 inches. Weight varies from 10 to 30 pounds. Fur color ranges from dark brown to nearly black with grey belly fur. The feet are webbed.

Otter are always found near water, although they can easily travel overland in a distinctive loping gait. They have a keen sense of smell, and they are famous for their ability to catch even the swiftest trout. Included in their diet are fish of all kinds, frogs, clams, crayfish, snakes, turtles, and small animals. The otter seems to have a dislike for mink and will kill a mink on contact.

Although considered a difficult animal to trap, it is probably more the case that otter are relatively scarce and their home range is large, sometimes covering 50 to 100 miles of shoreline. Where plentiful, they are no more difficult to trap than mink. Look for otter in wild areas containing many interconnecting streams, rivers, lakes, and ponds. They have a distinct liking for beaver ponds.

2

Planning
the Trapline

Prospecting our fall and winter trapline began the spring before, around late March or early April. Snow and ice were gone from the smaller creeks and water levels were near normal. As my son and I were walking along a creek bank, we noticed that the shorelines and bars of the sandy-bottomed creek were plastered with mink tracks.

"Don't be fooled by all these tracks, Dave," I pointed out. "I was here three weeks ago and there was only one mink track and one raccoon track. It hasn't rained since. These are probably the accumulated tracks of one or two mink. Still, it does look encouraging."

We used this early spring period to scout for the tracks, trails, and droppings of mink and raccoon along rivers, creeks, and lake shores. This was not so much serious prospecting as it was an attempt to get an idea of the numbers of animals in our area. We were new to this part of the state and I'd done only a limited amount of trapping here before.

"We can't hope to compete with trappers who have been trapping this country regularly," I told Dave one day. "When you hear of someone catching 25 or more mink, you can bet he's been trapping the same creeks and lake shores for a number of years. Some trappers will leave trap-anchoring wires in place from one year to the next. When the mink season opens, they merely attach one end of the wire to a trap, the other

9

end being anchored already. The trap is then set much as it was the year before. Of course, set locations will change over the years, but some locations, such as a road-side culvert, remain pretty much the same."

I later wished we had used the springtime more industriously because hiking in the cool weather through sparse vegetation was pleasant. All too soon, the weather warmed and hiking was made miserable by the heat, insects, and junglelike vegetation.

There were alternatives: inspecting road-side culverts for mink and raccoon sign was one; another was looking for fox and coyote sign in open fields and pastures and along old logging trails. But boating down the river was the most pleasant summer scouting we did.

We were towing our fishing boat on a tire-track trail that led to an access site on the river when I spotted a coyote. Dave and I hoped the sighting was a favorable omen for our day of scouting the river. This would be our last chance to do any scouting together until early fall, as Dave would be leaving the next day for a summer art course in another part of the state. A few hours later we had beached the boat on a river sand bar.

"When did it rain last?" I asked.

"About five nights ago, Dad, so all these raccoon tracks are fairly fresh."

In addition to fresh tracks, we found clamshells that had been opened and the contents devoured and raccoon droppings that were gritty with fragments of undigested crawfish. Raccoons favor large rivers over creeks because there are more of their favorite foods in rivers. Also, the animals can find large, hollow trees suitable for dens along river bottomlands.

I pointed out to Dave that mink prefer the little creeks and ditches to the big rivers, although we were finding a lot of mink signs, too. I noticed that the mink would run every tributary while the raccoons stayed close to the river. I knew that when the fall fruits ripened, whether wild or domestic, the raccoons would scatter over the countryside. Almost everyone who tries to raise sweet corn gets raided by raccoons.

I told Dave that I used to avoid catching raccoons because their fur value was so low. Now they were worth up to $60 apiece. It would pay to trap them.

We made a mistake early in the summer, though, in building set locations for mink and raccoon. I set a box cubby (described in Chapter 7) in a small spring where it entered a creek and later that summer high water, brought on by heavy rainfall, washed it away.

We had also narrowed trails used by mink. That is, we wedged sticks, logs, and rocks along trails to force the animals to move through a space

Figure 2–1 Sighting a coyote added to our enjoyment of a day of summer scouting.

just large enough to hold a steel trap and, we hoped, assure their capture. These preparations, too, were washed away. Early fall is a good time for making such preparations, although the weather and foliage may still be difficult to deal with. After the leaves have fallen and just prior to the trapping season is even better.

Gathering Equipment

While Dave was away that summer, I accumulated the equipment we would need for a fulltime trapline, a trapline in which we would trap a variety of animals. I started with a list of the following items:

1. Traps and snares
2. Trap dye
3. Pack sack or pack basket
4. Trap covers and stakes
5. Digging tool
6. Dirt sifter
7. Hatchet, knife, and wire clippers
8. Hip boots or waders
9. Dry dirt

11

10. Gloves	16. Lure bottles
11. Wire	17. Fleshing beam and tool
12. Flesh bait	18. Fleshing apron
13. Scent or lure	19. Tail splitter
14. Fish bait	20. Stretching boards
15. Fish oil	

I posted this list in a room in our basement, which was reserved for trapping supplies. As each item was acquired, I crossed it off the list. I'll discuss this list briefly. For more definitive information, see Chapter 12.

1. Traps and snares. For mink and raccoon trapping, I bought the No. 1½ Victor® coil-spring trap. This is an extremely strong trap, yet small and easy to conceal. It proved adequate as well for the occasional red fox that got into our raccoon sets. I remember one example of its holding power on raccoon.

Dave and I were each making a set for raccoon about 50 yards apart, and I was carrying a 20-foot length of beaver-cut tree trunk to my set to use as a trap drag. I could barely lift it. I told Dave later, "I might as well have staked the trap solid instead of to a drag. I doubt a raccoon could even budge that log."

About a week later, our daily trapline check revealed that the trap and tree trunk were gone. The set location looked as though a small bomb had gone off. The heavy tree trunk had been dragged for 20 yards through underbrush before trap, tree, and raccoon finally became entangled. The little coil spring was firmly in place on the toes of a 31 pound raccoon.

My other choice for a leg-hold trap was the No. 3 Oneida® jump, or under-spring, trap. This size would be necessary for such strong animals as coyote and beaver, though it is not a particularly good choice for fox. It can break a fox's leg bone, which helps the animal escape and causes unnecessary damage to it.

A large trap is an advantage in snow trapping. The larger the trap, the better it will function under a layer of crusted snow.

If it were not for coyote, I would have chosen the very popular Victor or the Blake & Lamb® No. 2 coil-spring trap. This size is an excellent trap for fox trapping, and many trappers use it as an all-around trap for fox, raccoon, and mink.

I bought two dozen No. 110 Conibear® traps for mink and muskrat and six No. 330 Conibear traps for beaver and otter. These are killer traps and while they do not always kill instantly, they are very adequate in water sets. Animals rarely escape.

Figure 2-2 This fat raccoon is held fast in a No. 1½ Victor coil-spring trap.

Figure 2-3 Dave and I set a 330 Conibear trap using the rope method described in the manufacturer's instructions. Later, I found I could set the trap by hand without ropes or setting tools.

PLANNING THE TRAPLINE

For deep snow trapping of coyote, I bought the No. 2 Swivel Kleflock Snare". This has a total length of three feet, although for greater ease in setting I'd have preferred a six-foot or even eight-foot snare. However, regulations in Minnesota restrict snare length to three feet.

I eventually accumulated 95 leg-hold traps, 30 Conibear (killer) traps, and 85 snares. We could have gotten by with less. I like the way my friend Charlie Mechley expressed it when he said, "I'd rather have 10 traps in well-made sets that I know will produce than 100 traps in haphazard sets."

Building sets attractive to your target animals is detailed in subsequent chapters. Proper and safe setting of the Conibear trap is shown in Chapter 12.

2. Trap dye. I bought commercial trap dye from Northwoods Trapline Supplies. Later in the season I needed more and was able to buy it at a local sporting goods store. Hardware and sporting goods stores seem to be stocking a greater variety of trapping supplies. I needed a little more than they had in stock, so I added tree bark to it. I used elm since I'd recently cut down a diseased elm tree in my yard. (See Chapter 13 for more details.)

3. Pack sack or pack basket. I was tempted to buy a pack basket popular with trappers in the East, and I wished I had. The pack sack I bought, while low in price, was a nuisance because the straps were always tearing loose. Dave used a Duluth pack with an empty cardboard box inside. This kept the top open and provided easy accessibility. He used pieces of cardboard to make compartments so bait and lure could be kept separate. The Duluth pack, which is very popular in our part of the country, is roomy, well made, and has heavy leather straps.

4. Trap covers and stakes. Trap covers keep the dirt concealing a trap from interfering with the trap's operation. I used plastic sandwich bags slipped under the jaws and over the pan of a trap. I had hoped to put the entire trap inside the bag and cover it with dirt, but when the jaws closed, the dirt covering was trapped between the jaws and prevented their closing properly.

I'd have preferred light canvas covers for early fall trapping. Condensation forms under the trap pan with the plastic cover and encourages rust (which has a distinctive odor).

A trip to a country dump resulted in a supply of trap stakes. I found an old baby crib and realized the hardwood slats around the sides of the crib would make good stakes.

5. Digging tool. I bought a digging tool from a trappers' supply house designed for making the popular dirt-hole set. Dave bought a small

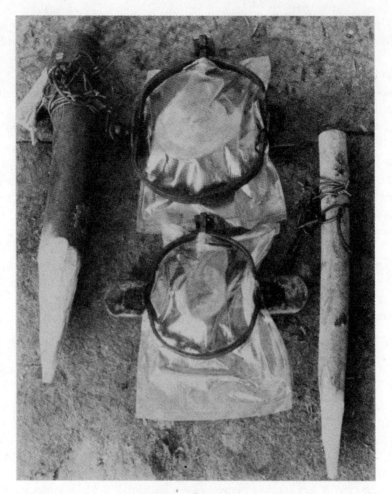

Figure 2–4 Plastic sandwich bags keep the space under the trap pans free of obstructions.

camper's shovel at a local store and narrowed the blade to about three inches. It worked fine.

6. Dirt sifter. I made several dirt sifters from old hardwood. They are simply a framework of wood with wire mesh in between. I made mine nine inches wide by ten inches long by two inches high, and used one-quarter-inch mesh. I'd have preferred higher sides, say four inches instead of two inches.

7. Hatchet, knife, and wire clippers. Like most outdoor enthusiasts, I had several hatchets and knives, but we did need another wire clipper. I also bought a knife to be used only for skinning. Our local hardware

Figure 2–5 Here I inspect one of several sizes of dirt sifters I made for our trapline.

stocked the Chicago Cutlery® brand of kitchen knives, and I bought model No. 62S. I'd noticed that our local fur buyer used that knife to skin whole animals that trappers had brought in and sold.

8. Hip boots or waders. I needed a new pair of hip boots and was tempted to buy waders since they are hard to beat for staying dry. But I opted for the hip boot, which is lighter in weight and easier to walk in. I'm not sure I made the best choice.

9. Dry dirt. Dry dirt is handy to use at dirt-hole sets when alternating freezing and thawing temperatures would normally put your traps out of order. I mixed dirt from our garden with sandier soil and spread it out on an old plywood panel and exposed it to the sun, occasionally raking it to expose lower layers. After drying, I put it in clean pails and stored it under our back porch.

Actually the dirt served a number of purposes, one of which was getting my truck out of slippery ruts that winter. A few handfuls under the rear wheels gave me the traction I needed.

10. Gloves. I used both rubber and cotton gloves, buying several pairs of the low-priced cotton ones so we could always have a clean pair. I liked wearing the cotton gloves, but the rubber ones were really superior and could be washed off in any creek or lake. When making sets where bait and lure were used, I always changed to the rubber gloves for handling it.

11. Wire. I bought fairly stiff, heavy wire for general trapping, probably around 12 gauge.

12. Flesh bait. The best bait we used I got from Charlie Mechley. This was domestic rabbit that Charlie had cut into chunks, allowed to become tainted, and then preserved in jars by adding ethylene glycol. (For details on this excellent fox and coyote bait, see Chapter 14.)

When we ran low on Charlie's bait, I shot three rabbits that had been raiding our garden all summer. After removing the entrails, I chopped them into 20 pieces each and put the pieces in a half-gallon plastic jar. Everything except the feet was cut into two-inch cubes, hair and all. It took only minutes to do on a chopping block and using a hatchet.

With the cover loose, I set the container of bait into a hole I'd dug in a shaded spot and covered it with dirt. The bait was slightly tainted within a week and just right for fox and coyote. It did the job on raccoon, too.

13. Lure. Charlie Mechley gave us a generous supply of top quality gland lure, made from real animal glands. Aside from preservative, it contained glands from timber wolf, coyote, fox, lynx, bobcat, and spring-caught male muskrat. This is primarily a lure for the wild canines and cats.

But there is no shortage of commercial lures or other trapping supplies. I had only to thumb through the pages of *Fur-Fish-Game* magazine to get the names and addresses of dozens of trappers' supply houses. I sent for catalogs from two of them—S. Stanley Hawbaker & Sons and E.J. Dailey's Lures & Baits. (See Sources of Supplies for addresses.) I bought fox, coyote, and mink urine from them as well as other trapping supplies.

Later in the season I needed more fox and mink urine and someone suggested I telephone Northwest Trapper's Supply, a Minnesota outfit that handles Hawbaker and Dailey lures.

14. Fish bait. All summer I talked about catching a mess of little bullheads, perch or some other easily caught fish and then freezing them to use later as bait for mink and raccoon. I never did, and I suspect our trapping suffered for it. Raccoon are particularly vulnerable to fish bait and the odor is one they can detect from a long distance.

15. Fish oil. Along with fish bait, fish oil is another item I neglected. (See Chapter 14 for making your own fish oil.) It makes a good lure for mink and raccoon. In fact, you can do without bait at a set if you use fish oil.

16. Lure bottles. The lure I got from Charlie Mechley came in a quart bottle, and I needed something smaller. The local druggist solved my problem. I bought one-ounce and four-ounce size empty bottles for about 5 cents each. The four-ounce size would be about right for homemade fish oil. Be sure to wash and boil any bottles in water to remove foreign odor before using.

17. Fleshing beam and tool. I made a fleshing beam from the crotch of a diseased elm tree that had to be cut down. This is just one of many ways to construct a fleshing beam. I bought the fleshing tool from a trapper's supply house.

18. Fleshing apron. Scraping the fat from pelts, especially fatty raccoon pelts, requires some kind of protection for your clothes. I'd hoped to buy a rubber apron of some kind but instead used an old raincoat.

19. Tail splitter. Our local fur buyer prefers that mink tails be split. It's hazardous to use a knife alone. The grooved rib from an old umbrella makes the job easier. The rib is inserted in the tail and a sharp knife is then slid down the groove, effectively splitting the tail. I fashioned a wooden handle for my splitter.

20. Stretching boards. With the exception of a dozen purchased wire stretchers for muskrat, I made my own stretching boards from wood that I found in dumps and abandoned farms. I made beautiful mink boards from the collapsed redwood sides of an old houseboat. I traced the desired shape from a commercial wooden mink stretcher. In making the fox and raccoon stretchers, I used a commercial wire stretcher to trace the desired shape.

In Chapter 15 I give details on skinning, fleshing, and drying pelts as well as measurements for building your own stretching boards. For now let me say that unless you have access to free wood, you might as well buy the wire commercial stretchers. They do an excellant job of drying pelts and the pelts dry much faster on them because there is greater air circulation.

At times I thought I was being overly conscientious in accumulating these items in midsummer, but time has a way of slipping by. Besides, I wanted to spend the early fall scouting our proposed trapline.

Another project was tidying our basement. We would be spending a lot of time there in the evenings skinning and fleshing pelts and I wanted to make it a pleasant place. I added a rustic touch by piling firewood along

Figure 2–6 Dave inspects one of our adjustable fur stretchers.

the walls. I also built simple frameworks to conceal less sightly areas of the basement and filled the frameworks with firewood. We have a barrel stove in the basement and a parlor stove upstairs in addition to our oil furnace. It was nice to sit by the basement barrel stove in the evenings and enjoy the warmth and the atmosphere. We fondly referred to the basement as our "trapper's shack."

Figure 2–7 We fondly referred to our basement as our "trapper's shack."

Scouting the trapline

By September, Dave and I had resumed scouting, or prospecting, the trapline. When the hunting seasons opened I carried my digging tool on my belt. I would frequently come upon a suitable site for a fox, coyote, or raccoon set while hunting grouse. Generally I would use the digging tool to do the preliminary work on what trappers call a dirt-hole set. This is an extremely effective set for catching animals on land, particularly fox and coyote. It is designed to imitate the hole and excavated dirt left by a fox or other animal when it buries food to be eaten at a later date. What makes it so effective is that wild animals of interest to the trapper love to rob each others' food cache.

When I killed a black bear over bait, I prepared several dirt-hole sets nearby because I knew that fox or coyote would eventually come around to investigate the bait that remained.

I liked to do the preliminary digging on dirt-hole sets before the trapping season as this meant less fuss when it came time to set traps. The more quickly sets can be made, the less human odor remains. Besides, it doesn't hurt for the animals you are after to get used to a set.

Later, as trapping season approached, we added bait and lure to these sets. One day Dave and I checked a dirt-hole set that I had baited and lured the week before. The sifted dirt in front of the hole showed coyote tracks, and the animal had been digging in the hole.

"No point in your getting any closer," I said to Dave. "I'll just add another piece of Charlie's bait and then we'll get away from here. I plan on setting a trap here around October 21, when the season on fox and raccoon opens. And I don't want to take any chance of spooking this one."

Coyote are unprotected in most states and we could trap them at any time, but there is no point in catching animals whose pelts are not yet prime. Younger animals prime later than adults, and the younger coyotes would not be in good condition until well into November.

We made preseason sets for raccoons by boat along a river in our area. Dave would run this river line while I took the truck and covered surrounding creeks, fields, and woodlands. We set up a tent along the river and used it as a base camp. It was an especially good base for Dave in running the river line. We spent many nights there rather than waste gas returning home.

Because of local regulations, we could not trap raccoon with sets made in the water until the mink and muskrat season opened November 4, and so we prepared land sets for raccoon. These were mostly dirt-hole sets,

Figure 2–8 Here I'm adding bait to a cubby built before the trapping season. Preparing and baiting sets before the season is one of the secrets to successful trapping.

but we also built cubbies and utilized hollow stumps and logs. We prebaited these with tainted rabbit flesh as we did those sets for fox and coyote. I would like to have used fish bait for those sets made principally for raccoon. Many sets were constructed with not only raccoon in mind, but for fox and coyote, too.

To determine what kind of animal has visited your set, dirt is sifted in front of a dirt-hole, cubby, hollow-stump, or hollow-log set. It isn't always easy, but sometimes you get a very clear, easy to identify footprint.

Due to high water all summer, we hadn't been able to do much scouting for mink. Now, as the trapping season drew near, the water levels were near normal, but we were deeply involved in preparing for the upcoming opening of fox and raccoon season.

Figure 2-9 I sift dirt in front of a cubby built before the season. Tracks of visiting animals will show clearly in the sifted dirt.

During all this roaming around the countryside scouting for mink, raccoon, fox, and coyote, we kept our eyes open for muskrat, beaver, and otter sign. After the snow came we hoped to find bobcat and fisher tracks. I've never attempted to trap such a variety of animals in one season before. The successful trappers I know stick to two or three species, which is certainly less confusing. But we were looking forward to a season of variety and, we hoped, adventure.

Finally, with trapping season drawing near, I prepared my traps in a solution of boiling water and commercial trap dye. Earlier in the summer I'd boiled the new traps to remove their protective coating of oil. Then I'd left them out in the weather to take on a coating of rust. Once a trap has rusted, it will take a good coat of dye and will better resist rust thereafter. The traps took on a deep blue-black color and a natural wood odor.

24

Figure 2–10 The sifted dirt in front of this dirt-hole is plastered with fox tracks. This will be a sure-fire set when the season opens.

Figure 2–11 Here's a very elaborate cubby I built into the side of a stream bank. Even without bait or lure, this is the kind of set no mink or otter could resist investigating.

Treating traps in this manner is necessary in order to trap fox, coyote, and mink. They can detect the odor of oil, steel, and rust from an untreated trap through many inches of soil. Once treated, the most cunning fox, coyote, or mink cannot detect the trap. (For more details, see Chapter 13.)

3
Fox and Raccoon

Opening day of the fox and raccoon trapping season was exhausting—I made 23 sets. Eighteen of those sets had been located and preliminary work done on them during preseason scouting trips.

I had almost abandoned one dirt-hole set I had dug in a small field of sparse weeds and grasses before the season, having seen fox tracks there, because preseason baiting never got a nibble. I decided to check the set one more time, though, and was glad I did because there were fresh fox tracks in front of the hole. I set a trap.

When I approached another dirt-hole set I'd made near the river, I found that a raccoon had not only been there and taken the bait but had dug holes everywhere as if expecting to find tid-bits buried in every corner of the woods. This was not unusual. Raccoon are ravenously hungry in early fall, not unlike their relative the black bear that stuffs its stomach in preparation for the long days of hibernation that lie ahead. (In more southerly climes, bear and raccoon will retire to dens for only short periods or not at all.)

Dave was busy, too. While I was running the auto trapline, he was setting traps from our campsite on the river. He used our old 14-foot fishing boat and ancient Johnson five-and-one-half horsepower outboard motor. Motoring upstream from camp that first day, he set traps in locations prepared before the season and made new sets.

Figure 3–1 By the time we set up camp on the eve of running our trapline, Dave already knows where he will be setting the first of his river traps.

A few nights later Dave and I sat in front of a campfire and watched the stars come out. It gets dark early in the fall, and soon we could see only the outline of trees on the opposite shore of the river. We talked for hours, describing to one another the events we'd experienced during the first three days of the season.

Because a lot of this was new to him, Dave had a particularly interesting time of it. His first stop was just around the bend from our camp at a grassy field that borders the river. We'd prepared a dirt-hole set along the edge of the field in early October. The set had been approached by both a raccoon and a fox.

Figure 3–2 As storm clouds build, Dave prepares a dirt-hole set for fox and raccoon.

"I wanted that first set to be a good one," Dave told me. "I beached the boat, waded in the river to wash away any foreign odor from my hip boots, and scrambled up the bank with my Duluth pack loaded with everything I would need: trap, stake, hatchet, bait, gland lure, fox urine, gloves, dirt sifter, and trap cover."

Dave made the set quickly, then stepped back for a final inspection. A hole, roughly three to four inches in diameter, angled into the ground for six inches. The hole was in one corner of a triangular patch of sifted dirt. The dirt looked as if it had been scattered there by an animal in digging the hole. Trap and stake were concealed under that dirt.

He added more bait to the hole and dropped a two-inch twig dipped in gland lure beside it. Then he sprinkled fox urine over the dirt where the trap was concealed and the grass where he'd crouched while making the set.

29

A MODERN TRAPLINE

Most of the sets Dave made that first day were dirt-hole sets, or variations of it. In some cases, he simply tossed bait in the back of a hollow log, tree, or stump and set a trap in front. Those sets were made primarily for raccoon. He also set traps in the cubbies we had built for raccoon along the river before season. These were three-sided and had a roof of sorts. We built them from available materials such as logs, rocks, or old boards. Bait was tossed in back and a trap set in the entrance.

Altogether, Dave set 28 traps, and eagerly looked forward to checking them the next day.

"I could hardly wait," Dave related. "My first two sets, both dirt-hole sets, were empty. But it didn't bother me. I told myself they just needed more time. Then I checked a cubby set. Empty. The trap was knocked out of the way at a hollow-log set. I began to wonder. . . ."

Motoring to his next set, he landed the boat where a small rivulet entered the river. He had baited a hollow stump upstream along this rivulet, figuring a raccoon might follow it and discover the set. There had been raccoon droppings where the rivulet entered the river. Dave was just getting out of the boat when he heard the distinct sound of a rattling trap chain. He turned in the direction of the sound and stood dumbfounded, staring into the eyes of a red fox.

The fox, he finally realized, was in a trap—his trap. The trap was wired to a popple drag, four-inches thick by three feet long. The fox had pulled it down to the river. Dave guessed it must be a young one to have approached a set made for raccoon in a hollow stump, but after dispatching it with his .22 rifle, he found it to be an adult female. Very pale and with a large bushy tail.

The next set was a dirt-hole set along the edge of a field. The sun was getting warm and he slipped off his wool coat as he climbed the steep bank from the river. Crossing an old barbed wire fence, he noticed a dark blob where he knew the set should be. Breaking into a fast walk he decided it was probably just a skunk . . . but no, it was a raccoon, a really big one. All of a sudden, Dave told me later, his knees felt wobbly and he couldn't stop smiling. He'd done things right.

Dave caught two red fox and a raccoon that day. Not bad when you consider this is not ideal fox country to start with.

Red fox are more abundant in open farm country. Our area is heavily wooded and more conducive to coyotes, or brush wolves, as some people call them. Still, foxes often appear in fringe areas and they thrive in the hay fields and pastures. When fur prices are low, they multiply like rabbits.

Figure 3–3 After making a set for raccoon in the cubby shown in the foreground, Dave prepares to motor further upstream on the river trapline.

Figure 3–4 Dave heads back to the river after making a set for red fox along a powerline clearing.

Figure 3–5 Dave poses with the pelts of the first two foxes he caught.

A few days later Dave and I launched my 17-foot canoe on a very small stream in our area. There was enough water to float the canoe, although we had to pull and shove it over an occasional fallen tree or logjam.

We had done no preseason scouting or any preliminary work on sets along this waterway. We made every set from scratch. We were looking for raccoon primarily, but there was always the hope of catching a fox. And we made each set with as much care as we would in trapping the more elusive red fox.

Hollow-stump sets

I made the first set in the base of a hollow stump. (There was an opening in one side of the stump forming a natural cubby.) I used my digging tool to scrape leaves and rubble out of the hollow and away from the entrance. I scratched right down to the bare ground in a fan-shape outside the entrance, as if an animal had stuck its paw into the hollow stump and raked out the rubble.

Then I dug a bed for the trap in front of the entrance. It was deep enough so that the trap, when set, would be slightly below ground level. I put the dirt and rubble I'd dug from the trap bed into my dirt sifter. Then I set a No. 1½ double coil-spring trap, adjusted the pan to a hair trigger, and slipped a plastic sandwich bag under the jaws and over the pan to keep dirt from getting under it. I'd already wired the trap chain to a five-foot length of four-inch thick alder.

With the trap set in the bed and the trap cover in place, I sifted dirt over it until it was barely covered. Too much covering on a trap prevents it from operating properly. I raked leaves over the trap chain and wire and tossed bait into the back of the hollow, covering it lightly with leaves. The latter was done to make it appear buried. I had a little fox urine along and sprinkled this around. While I did not use any, a commercial raccoon lure would have added a nice touch.

I knew I didn't have to be so fussy with a raccoon set. While it is an intelligent animal, the raccoon is not very trap-wise, and it is greedy. Nevertheless, it doesn't take much effort to do it right and this can pay off should a fox or other elusive animal come sniffing around. Besides, it pays to stay in the habit of being careful in making sets. When you are doing things right even the super trap-wise coyote are easily caught. And believe me, you have to do things right to trap coyote. Foxes aren't easily fooled, either. Make one little mistake and a skinny five-month-old fox will laugh at your set and scamper off into the sunset.

We had our usual problems that day. For one thing, it is hard to get enough dirt to cover your trap from a trap bed dug in typical woodland soil. I usually had to do some additional digging elsewhere before I found enough real dirt to sift over the trap.

When sets are made near water, the ground may be damp. This is when a supply of dry dirt comes in handy. Damp earth may freeze and prevent the trap working. We had a pail full of dry dirt in the canoe and used it when there was not sufficient dry material to cover a trap.

Sometimes the opening in a hollow stump, tree, or cubby is so wide that a raccoon investigating the set may miss stepping in the trap. We narrowed the openings with sticks and rocks. Sometimes I would take two sticks, about as big around as my finger and a foot or so long, and push each into the ground on each side of the trap. Each stick would angle slightly under the trap. These guide sticks then looked like the letter "V" with the trap at the bottom and just inside them. It pays to do everything possible to guide an animal into your trap.

Because the raccoon is a powerfully built animal with tapered feet, some are able to pull out of a trap if it is solidly anchored. So, we used drags at some of the sets we made that day. A drag is a length of log or tree branch wired to the end of the trap chain and light enough that the animal can pull it. A drag of three feet or more will continually snag a brush, preventing the raccoon from getting a solid pull. The raccoon will rarely get more than 100 feet before tangling up in brush permanently, and by then it would be too tired to fight any longer. I don't believe we had one travel more than 60 feet from the set location.

You can add to the drag's effectiveness and cause a raccoon to tangle in brush sooner by adding a two-foot length of wire between the end of the trap chain and the drag. A length of 16-gauge electric fence wire will normally do the job, but it doesn't hurt to use a double strand. Use three-to five-inch diameter hardwood (oak, maple, and so on) for drags. These should be at least three to four feet long. I sometimes used drags that were six inches thick at one end and 15 to 20 feet long, whatever was handy.

I prefer to stake the trap solid when making dirt-hole sets for raccoon along the edges of open fields where there is a chance of catching fox in the set. (This set is described in detail later in this chapter.) Fox are sometimes spooked by a drag lying near the set. We found that a long, slender stake will hold better than a short, fat one. We shortened the trap chain to prevent raccoon or fox making high jumps and possibly pulling loose from the trap.

Cubby Sets

Dave and I continued making sets as we canoed the small stream. We built a couple of cubby sets in addition to those we made in hollow stumps and trees. One was built where Dave and I followed a trickle of water back to where it drained a swamp. Dave noticed two big logs on the ground and suggested that we fashion a cubby by laying some smaller logs across and between the logs.

Cubbies are nothing more than artificial hollow logs and stumps. Traps are set in the entrances. This day we baited the cubbies with canned sardines. They give off a very strong fishy odor and are attractive to raccoon.

We ended the day with ten sets made. The last two were a dirt-hole set and, a short distance away, a hollow-tree set. Raccoon sign was so heavy in this last spot that we couldn't resist putting in two sets. In fact, we sometimes found it pays to really saturate a spot to insure catching an animal. It is exasperating to paddle a great distance or walk a long ways to find that an animal has managed to side-step your set, and knowing that if you had one or two more sets nearby you would probably have caught it.

In this case it took three trips before we caught the raccoon. The first time I checked those last two sets, my 12-year old daughter Tracy was with me. She had spent the night with Dave and me at the river camp and then helped me paddle the canoe upstream on this small river. The trap in the dirt-hole set had been unearthed and tipped over. It was still set, but it was upside down, and the bait had been taken. The set in the hollow tree which was out of sight behind more trees was not touched.

I told Tracy, "I know a raccoon isn't smart enough to do this on purpose, yet those are certainly raccoon tracks."

The next time Dave was with me. We caught a raccoon in the second of the ten sets we'd originally made, a hollow-tree set.

"Maybe we'll catch the one that tipped over our trap at the dirt-hole set," I said to Dave. I was feeling confident, having caught the raccoon and, around the next bend in the river, having seen a mink bounding along the shoreline.

But on reaching the set, I was astounded to find the trap turned over again and the bait gone. I hurried to the other set in the hollow tree, but it hadn't been touched. I guessed the second set was downwind of the raccoon's route. Once again we reset the trap at the dirt-hole.

We should have guessed by then what the problem was, but we always seemed to be in a hurry during those early days of the season and

Figure 3–6 A woodland dirt-hole set for raccoon.

didn't take the time to think this one out. Or, if we suspected, didn't act.

The third time I was alone. None of the sets had produced and I was feeling depressed. When I approached the troublesome dirt-hole set and found the trap set off and on its side I felt even worse. This time the bait had not been taken. I suspected that the traps snapping closed frightened the animal.

By now it was obvious that there was food or lure odor on the trap and the raccoon was digging it up thinking it was good to eat. Perhaps a drop

37

of sardine oil had spilled on the dirt covering the trap. We'd had some sardines along on that first trip. The trap might have contacted the odor from one of our pack sacks. We tried to keep bait and lure separate from the other equipment but we certainly weren't perfect.

This was not an isolated case. In some instances traps were knocked out of position or tipped over because the raccoon was so eager to get a free meal it started digging before it reached the bait hole. Dainty they aren't.

The solution here was to replace the tainted trap with a clean one. But first I wanted to check the set in the hollow tree.

The first thing I noticed was the lack of bark near the base of the hollow tree, and then I saw scratch marks. The drag was gone! The second set had finally payed off.

It was easy to follow the raccoon's progress as it pulled and fought its way through the underbrush. Yet it was a relief to see its thickly furred back showing over the top of a log, the soft outline of its fur rising and falling slowly. It was sound asleep.

I carry a Smith & Wesson revolver in the old Model 34 with four-inch barrel and load it with .22 short ammunition. It is a handy tool for killing trapped animals; I recommend it.

Unfortunately the law in my state makes it illegal to kill game animals with a handgun. The only animal on my trapline I can use it on is coyote. So I carry a .22 rifle most of the time and now I used it to kill the raccoon.

I have my rifle and revolver sighted-in to hit the point of aim at 15 feet with .22 short ammunition. The raccoon was only half awake when I sighted on the center of its forehead and fired. There was much thrashing about and loss of blood but death, I knew, was instantaneous.

Blind Sets

Finally the time came when we could make water sets for raccoon. We made blind sets mostly. That is, we set traps where we believed the raccoons would walk. No bait or lure was used.

Any spot where a raccoon has to travel is a potential blind set. A log crossing a stream is excellent. It should be checked for scratch marks and droppings. If these are present, a notch should be cut on top of the log for a trap bed. The trap is then covered with moss or fine pulverized rotted wood.

I'd made such a set and one day found a red squirrel in the trap; or rather, what remained of it. A mink, whose fresh dropping was nearby, had killed and eaten it. I reset the trap and put what remained of the squirrel near it. The mink season was open, and I hoped to catch it. The next time around I had a big fat raccoon in the trap. I never did catch that mink.

When we walked a stream bank or cruised near shore in a boat or canoe, we looked for spots that would narrow a raccoon's travels. A steep bank or a large tree stump often blocks a raccoon. This forces the animal to wade or swim around the obstruction. The point where the raccoon enters the water is where we set our trap. Traps would be set firmly in the mud or sand bottom under one to two inches of water. No covering was used. Generally the trap chain was wired to a stout tree root.

Baited Sets

Because bait is so effective in luring raccoons, we made some baited sets along the edge of stream banks. We looked for naturally recessed spots, such as the space under exposed tree roots, and put bait in back and the trap in front in such a way that the raccoon must pass over it to reach the bait. Guide sticks were important.

We also made artificial bait holes. These were usually made at a point where shallow water touches a steep bank. A hole was dug straight into the bank with the mouth low enough to allow water to flow at least part way into the hole. The hole was about one foot deep and eight inches in diameter. The bait was placed in back of the hole, and a trap guarded the entrance. Lure was sometimes used as an added incentive. Both mink and raccoon will tumble to this set, and it is not uncommon to pick up a muskrat.

As we continued to trap raccoon, we became concerned about the job we were doing in fleshing their pelts. Dave thought we might be taking off too much flesh because we could see hair roots. We asked Charlie Mechley, who used to buy fur, and found our fears were unfounded. In fact, he pointed out where we could have taken off more. You must flesh raccoons right down to the hair roots. If you can flesh them clean, up to a line even with or slightly below the ears, you will have done well. The area around the head and shoulders is tough and gristly. Still, we did our best to scrape it clean. A word of warning: don't work with too sharp a fleshing tool. After inflicting several cuts in one pelt, I took a file to my new fleshing tool and rounded its too-sharp edge.

Figure 3–7 This raccoon was caught in a dirt-hole set made
along the shore of a river.

Figure 3–8 Some of our early-season catch.

As the season progressed, so did the primeness of the raccoon's fur. The flesh side was becoming cream colored, and we could no longer see hair roots. The fact is, raccoons in this part of the country do not prime fully until mid-November. Unfortunately, many are already hibernating by then.

Culvert Sets

On my auto trapline I made numerous sets for raccoon and mink in culverts. These are good set locations because they channel the movement of these animals as efficiently as they do a flow of water. When a roadbed is reached, it is just natural for the mink or raccoon to stick to the water. A culvert or bridge is a natural funnel for furbearers.

I usually made sets as close to the mouth of a culvert as possible. This is usually the most restricted spot in an animal's passage. Even a culvert, though, must often be narrowed down to insure the mink or raccoon

41

Figure 3–9 A culvert set.

steps directly over the trap. Rocks and logs found in the vicinity were used for this restriction. This is a blind set and no bait or lure was used.

By mid-November there was snow and cold and most of the raccoons had retired to dens, so I was surprised to find that a roving raccoon had escaped from a culvert set. It had chewed almost half of a six-foot drag to a narrow frazzle. The wire around the drag had not been twisted on very tightly and had slipped off the chewed end. I followed the raccoon's tracks in the snow. The length of wire still attached to the trap had many kinks and twists in it and became entangled when the raccoon entered a thicket.

I had foolishly forgotten to bring ammunition for either my rifle or revolver. It was almost dark, and I should have left the raccoon and returned the next day. The raccoon was sleeping soundly and might even have gone into a state of hibernation right where it was. Instead, I tried to kill it with a club. My first blow was a glancing one and the raccoon

Figure 3–10 When this big raccoon turned on me, I was sure it would chew its way
right up my leg!

screamed with rage and tore loose from the brush that had been restraining it. I turned to run and slipped in the snow. Raccoon, I knew, bite like an out-of-control jack hammer. I yelled and rolled over and over to get away from that large and very agitated animal.

But instead of chewing its way up my leg, it dove for an opening at the base of a hollow tree and began climbing up the hollow. I caught the end of the wire still attached to the trap chain and got a demonstration of raccoon power. For a moment I feared the wire would cut through my mitten and then my hand. Suddenly the wire went slack—the raccoon had pulled free.

I reset the trap at the base of the tree and another in the culvert. That night a highly educated, but none the worse for wear, raccoon crawled out of a hole high in the tree. It came down the opposite side of the tree from where my trap was set. It avoided the culvert where I'd first caught it and ran off into the moonlit night.

One thing kept me from feeling too badly when I discovered all this the next day—the trap in the culvert held a huge buck mink. Not a bad booby prize.

While the raccoons had called it quits for the year, the red foxes, what few there were, continued to be relatively active, although they will restrict their activities during severely cold weather. In this part of the country, it gets to 20, 30, and even 40 degrees below zero Fahrenheit. Foxes move very little during such cold snaps. But when it warms, it's nice to have good sets waiting.

Dirt-hole sets

Most of the foxes that are trapped each year are trapped in the fall months before deep snow and cold weather. And most fox trappers rely almost entirely on the dirt-hole set, including those who are after the grey fox. It takes only minutes to make the set and when you do it right, it is almost always effective. You *do* have to do it right, though, and just as important, you have to make it where the fox will find it and be willing to approach it. It really isn't too difficult; the hard part is describing it. The following list may help:

1. Pick a location.
2. Choose a back-stop.
3. Remove sod.
4. Dig the hole.
5. Dig the trap bed.

Figure 3–11 Here I'm preparing a set for fox along the edge of a field. The terrain is perfect for the dirt-hole set.

6. Pound in the trap stake.
7. Set the trap.
8. Change gloves.
9. Add bait and lure.
10. Change gloves.
11. Retrieve equipment.
12. Brush out tracks.
13. Add fox urine.

Now let's take them one at a time:

1. Pick a location. Red foxes, because of their timid nature, prefer open terrain. They often sleep on high knolls where they have a view of the surrounding countryside. When they hunt it is usually along the edge of cover. Hunting the edges allows a fox to hunt prey and still keep an eye out for danger.

Trappers have found that the dirt-hole works best when made in a fairly open field and away from high grass, trees, large rocks, and stumps. I don't think it pays to get too far out in a field. Twenty to fifty feet from the edge of a woodlot, marsh, or brushy fencerow is plenty. We sometimes made our sets even closer. Incidentally, the closer you make the set to cover, the greater the odds of adding a raccoon to your catch.

We try to make our sets upwind of where we believe a fox will be traveling. The dirt-hole set is not very noticeable. The fox is built close to the ground and its field of view is limited. What catches its attention is the odor of bait and lure.

Some of our sets for fox were in heavily forested terrain. We followed logging trails into those areas and made sets in small clearings that edged the trails. Foxes, more than any other of the common furbearers, like to travel where the going is easy. They run for long distances down these logging trails, so to construct a set downwind from a trail is folly. A northwest wind is common in our area and I usually made my sets in a northwesterly direction from the trail. I also bracketed a trail with sets on either side.

One day I made a dirt-hole set for fox in a hay field and about 30 feet from woodlands of second-growth aspen. I hadn't seen any fox sign here but it looked "foxy," the kind of terrain where mice were thick and rabbits abundant. I approached the spot I had in mind wearing hip boots, scuffing the soles in some loose dirt, and then spraying them lightly with fox urine before getting too close. Charlie Mechley used to keep a pair of galoshes big enough to fit over his hiking boots in a big plastic bag in the

46

back of his jeep. He would carry this bag and the boots for 50 feet or so from his jeep and then remove the galoshes and put them on. He would then proceed to a set location and either make a set or check an old one. When returning to his jeep, he would stop about 50 feet away, remove the galoshes, and put them back in the plastic bag.

A lot of bother? Maybe. But Charlie's galoshes were free of foreign odor and Charlie caught a lot of foxes. The point is to have your boots either odor-free or smelling of something that does not frighten the foxes or make them suspicious.

2. Choose a back-stop. A back-stop, or backing, can be a rock, clump of grass, small bush, or anything that blocks the back side of a dirt-hole set so a fox would be inclined to approach the set from the front, where the trap would be. (The trap, of course, is treated and free of all but a wood odor.) The backing has to be small enough that the fox can see over and around it. The whole point in making sets in open fields and clearings is the fox can see all around and have no fear of being ambushed. In this case I made the set against a hump in the ground that was shaped like half of a grass-covered basketball.

3. Remove sod. With my digging tool, which looks like a miniature shovel with a blade less than three inches wide, I cut out a triangular-shaped piece of sod about one foot on a side. One corner of the triangle was against the back-stop. I tried to work the sod free of the ground in one piece, but it crumbled. I picked up the pieces and shook loose dirt from each one over the excavated area and then tossed what was left as far as I could.

4. Dig the hole. Next I dug a hole about two to three inches wide and six inches deep in the corner by the backing at a 45 degree angle under the back-stop. I put this dirt in my sifter. I now had a triangular-shaped patch of dirt with a hole in one corner, and all that remained was the placement of trap and bait.

5. Dig the trap bed. Directly in front of the hole I dug a bed for the trap. I put this dirt in the sifter, also. I set a trap in the bed to to see how it would fit. The trap dog, or trigger mechanism, should be about one inch from the edge of the hole. When lightly covered with sifted dirt, I wanted the whole thing to be level with the surrounding dirt.

6. Pound in the trap stake. I removed the trap and set the trap stake in the center of the bed. The stake was already wired to the trap chain by the fourth link from the trap. I pounded it into the ground completely out of sight.

7. Set the trap. Because the chain had been attached to the stake close

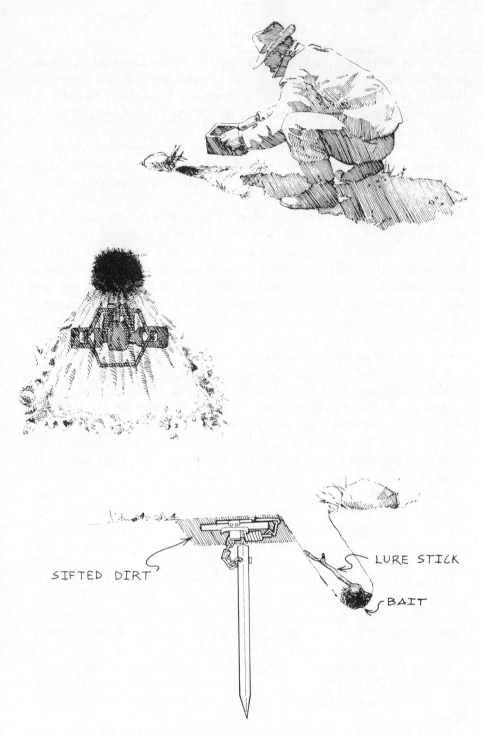

SIFTED DIRT

LURE STICK

BAIT

Figure 3–12 A dirt-hole set for fox.

to the trap, the trap now fit in the hole with almost no slack in the chain. This would prevent a fox from making high leaps and possibly pulling free.

I cocked the trap and slipped a plastic sandwich bag under the trap jaws and over the trap pan. I adjusted the pan to a hair trigger, and then pressed the trap firmly into the soil. I didn't want it to rock even if a fox stepped only on one corner of a jaw.

Next I sifted the dirt in the sifter over the trap. When I finished there was a slight pyramid of dirt directly over the trap pan. I leveled this with the blade of my hatchet.

8. Change gloves. The next thing I did was change gloves. I put on a pair that I reserved for only one thing—handling bait and lure.

9. Add bait and lure. With a piece of stiff wire, I speared a piece of bait from the bait jar and dropped it into the hole, being careful not to spill juice on the buried trap. I then broke off a two-inch twig, dipped it into my bottle of gland lure, and dropped it into the hole beside the bait.

10. Change gloves. I removed the gloves worn for handling bait and lure, pinning them to the outside of my pack sack. I slipped on the pair reserved for handling traps and other equipment.

11. Retrieve equipment. It's frustrating to leave your hatchet or some other item of equipment at a set location. Take the time to check.

12. Brush out tracks. An old broom stub is a handly item for straightening the grass where you have crouched while making a set. In this case I simply used my digging tool.

13. Add fox urine. I took a step back and reached for the bottle of fox urine. I wasn't concerned about getting any of it on my gloves because it is a very natural odor to the fox. In fact, I'd rubbed some into the gloves earlier. I sprayed the spot where the trap was buried and where I'd been crouched while making the set. You really can't use too much of it. Trapper's supply houses usually refer to it as "suspicion remover."

I planned to add more gland lure to the set in three or four days, but it wasn't necessary because two days later I caught a fox. The odor left by a trapped fox is super scent for luring more fox. It didn't concern me in the least that the fox had made a mess of things. I simply spruced up the set as best I could, dug out the hole which had been plugged, and reset the trap.

There had been some blood in disposing of the fox. I'd scooped up the dirt in those spots and tossed it as far as I could. Blood is food to a fox and I didn't want any successive foxes digging for it. More often than not this results in a sprung trap rather than a trapped fox.

The dirt-hole set can be used after snow and cold weather come if the dirt can be kept dry. We had no problems with this, having saved dry dirt from the previous summer. Antifreeze solutions can also be used. These are available from trapper's supply houses, usually with urine added, and can be sprayed on a set to prevent freezing. You can make your own from ethylene glycol, the same liquid used in the recipe for preserving fox bait (see chapter 14). Mix a little fox urine with it.

The best way I found for carrying dry dirt to a set was in a canvas bag inside of my pack sack. The bag was of World War I vintage and was originally designed to carry mess gear. It had a draw string on top and held more than enough dirt. I got it from Charlie Mechley, who carried it on his trapline for many, many years. You might find something similar at an Army-Navy surplus store.

When the snow is a foot or more deep, I'm inclined to leave my traps at home and switch over to the self-locking steel snare. I couldn't do it on this trapline, however, as only coyotes could be snared legally. (See Chapter 5 if you are interested in snaring fox. The methods are almost identical, and I give some specifics in regards to taking foxes with snares.)

Trail sets

I knew that foxes could be trapped in trails using steel leg-hold traps instead of snares, but I had never done it. Then my old trapping mentor Charlie Mechley came to the rescue.

"Find where the fox steps over a stick or root in the trail," Charlie said, "and make your set right in the fox's footprint in the snow. Start by scooping away the snow with your digging tool in this spot, and put the snow in your dirt sifter. Scoop out enough snow so when the trap is set, the trap pan will be slightly below the depth of the original footprint.

"It pays," Charlie continued, "to use a fairly large trap. The bigger the better for breaking through crusted snow. Those No. 3 jump traps you have should do it. They're bigger than you need for fall trapping of foxes, but just right for winter trapping.

"The next thing to do is lay a piece of wax paper in the trap bed. Then take another piece and slip it under the trap jaws and over the pan. Now set the trap in the bed. Pick up your dirt sifter and sift the snow you dug back over the trap and fill in everything to a level even with the surrounding snow. You don't have to sift the snow, but it seems to sit more lightly when you do, like freshly fallen snow.

"Now take from your pack sack the front foot and leg of a red fox, saved from one of those you caught in the fall. Press the foot into the

50

Figure 3–13 Red fox trapped in a dirt-hole set. This set was made near the edge of a cow pasture.

Figure 3–14 My daughter Tracy carries out a red fox caught in a trail set.

snow *directly* over the trap pan. The next time it comes through, the fox will step in the track and you've got him."

I knew it would work. After many years of snaring foxes and coyotes, I was well aware of their tendency to trail; that is, they step exactly in their previous footprints the next time they come by. They are especially prone to do so when traveling from one patch of woods to another. Foxes will scamper all over a woodlot or swamp, but when they move on to another, they follow the same trail. True, it doesn't look like a trail since there is, seemingly, only a single track. But that single track has been trod many times. Even when a snowfall fills them in, the fox's feet land almost unerringly in the same prints.

Charlie told me he liked to dry a fox foot with the claws protruding. Once he removed the leg bone and replaced it with a length of broom handle. He used the foot in fall trapping to make scratch marks at dirt-hole sets and to make a footprint directly over the trap pan.

How do you keep from setting off the trap when making a print over the pan? (See Chapter 5 for details on fine-tuning a trap.) Actually, it takes about two pounds of pressure to set off the trap, and when it goes off, it goes off immediately. This makes for higher catches on an animal's foot because it has its full weight on the trap when it snaps shut. Try it with one of your traps and see what I mean.

I used the trail set almost exclusively throughout January, the final month of the season. It worked especially well because we had continuous below-freezing temperatures, resulting in dry, uncrusted snow conditions. Sometimes I anchored the trap to a nearby tree trunk with wire. At other sets I used a short, hardwood drag pushed out of sight in the snow. I usually brushed over the spot with a pine bough and brushed out my footprints for several yards.

In deep snow it may be impossible to find where a fox is stepping over a stick or root because everything is buried. In this case, to help ensure the fox's staying in his tracks, lay a dead stick no more than one inch in diameter in the snow and a few inches in front of the fox's track.

There are more sets that will take foxes, but those described here and used by Dave and myself will see you through a successful season. Additional sets for fox can be found in my book, *The Complete Book of Trapping*.

4

Mink and Muskrat

The mink and muskrat season opened November 4. This was a late opener for these species in the northern part of the state—normally the season would have opened a week earlier. I wasn't too concerned about muskrat, but the late opener could seriously affect the mink trapping. If winter came early, we would have less than two weeks of open water trapping before the creeks, rivers, and lake shores froze. Trapping mink after freeze-up is difficult.

The best way to catch mink, I think, is to cover a lot of brooks, creeks, water-filled ditches, and lake shores with traps. Almost every little trickle of water has at least one mink following it, and the more of those you cover with good sets, the more mink you're going to catch. So why, I asked myself, am I paddling the canoe up this stream again? This was the same small stream where we has so much trouble catching the raccoon that was tipping over our trap. I knew full well why. Almost every trip on this stretch of the little river I'd seen a mink. One day I'd seen two. Besides, I still had sets for raccoon along the river and some of those I wanted to switch from land to water.

In addition to moving some of the dry-land raccoon sets to the water and making sets for mink, I planned to set traps for muskrat. On earlier trips I'd noted a number of underwater bank den entrances and logs that were dotted with their droppings.

54

A blind curiosity set

The first two traps I set combined a blind set and a curiosity set for mink. I'd noticed the location a few weeks before: an immense but thoroughly rotted stump sprawled over a sloping bank, its roots jutting down into the water. I set one trap under one inch of water in a narrow channel between the roots and the bank. This is a "classic" blind set for mink since they almost always will investigate such a narrow passageway.

Figure 4–1 Dave applies a few drops of mink urine to a set made at water's edge.

The other trap I set within the rotted interior of the stump, where a six-inch diameter hole had formed. How could I miss? If a mink came along the top of the bank it would surely be curious about the hole within the rotted stump. And if it came traipsing along in the shallow water by shore, I'd catch it for certain in the blind set in the water. Added to all this was the fact the set was on the *inside* of a bend in the river. When they come to a bend in a river, creek, water-filled ditch, or tiny brook, mink will run the inside of the bend. Probably because it shortens their route.

Oddly enough, neither of those traps produced. And I still don't know why. I could make some educated guesses, and I'm not referring to the education I received in 30 years of part-time mink trapping. I mean the education I got that winter while trying to trap mink in deep snow, sub-zero temperatures, and frozen creeks when every one else had enough sense to pull their traps. Every mistake I made was written in the snow. My biggest mistake was in not taking every precaution to insure that passing mink would land squarely on the pan of my waiting trap.

It would be different if they were slow, plodding creatures who took their time when something caught their interest. They are, however, highstrung, highly excitable creatures who rarely walk when they can hop, jump, or leap. The normal loping gait of a mink on land can leave an 18-inch gap between footprints. The trap pan of a No. 1½ double coil-spring is a little over two inches wide. Unless you do it right, you can miss a mink each and every time it comes to your set. But more on that later. Because my next set was made for that wonderfully cooperative creature called a muskrat.

Den sets for muskrat

On earlier trips I'd seen several trenches in the bottom that led to muskrat den entrances under a foot or so of water. The trenches looked a little lighter in color than the sand- and silt-covered bottom and had been formed by the comings and goings of the occupants of the dens. I beached the canoe and cut a half-dozen aspen saplings to use for stakes. With these in the front of the canoe I looked closely for that first underwater den entrance. The den itself would be high and dry somewhere in the river bank. When I saw it, I let the canoe drift into shore as I prepared a trap and trap stake.

The aspen saplings I'd cut for stakes were four to five feet long. I put the end of one through the chain ring and spring of a No. 110 Conibear trap. This smallest of the killer-type traps is ideal for mink and muskrat. I positioned the trap about one foot from the bottom of the stake and held it in place with soft wire wrapped around the spring and stake. Then I positioned the canoe over the den entrance. I set the end of the stake into the water next to the den entrance and pushed it into the soft bottom until the trap was aligned with the entrance.

At least I hoped it was aligned. Mud and silt billowed up as I set it in position and I couldn't see. Instead of wasting time waiting for the water to clear, I left. I planned to stop on the way back and check to see if it was sitting correctly. Two hours later I did just that and found I had to reset the trap because I'd already caught a muskrat.

Forced water sets

Most of the sets I made that day were blind sets for mink and muskrat, that is, I set traps where I believed the animals would step. I remembered that Charlie Mechley had told me that mink are more land animals than water animals and they will step in water only if forced to. "They lope along a creek edge following what little beach there is and never get their feet wet unless they have too," Charlie said. "A tree trunk or rock jutting out from the bank can force them to take to the water in order to get around it. Set your trap in the water. You can make an artificial obstruction with sticks set in a row from the bank out to the water's edge. Set your trap under one to two inches of water just beyond the last stick."

I was to see many examples that showed Charlie was right. And when the weather turned cold and ice formed along the edges of creeks and lake shores, the mink would run for long distances on the "beach" of ice. Sometimes it was hard to find set locations under such conditions because the ice formed on the obstructions, too. But the ice was slow to form where there were riffles and sets could be made there.

I made sets for muskrat where they had been crawling out of the water onto rocks and floating logs. Many of the blind sets made for mink and raccoon were potential muskrat sets.

Another log set

I made one set for mink that was a little different from any I'd ever made before. I set a trap on top of a tree trunk that was half submerged in the river. I'd set traps on trees and logs that spanned small creeks before, and I'd set traps on the ends of logs where muskrat had been crawling out of the water, but this was a huge tree trunk that spanned half of the river. I made the set because those mink I'd been seeing seemed to have an affinity for running out on these big trees that had fallen into the water.

57

TRAPS WIRED TO
ROCKS IN DEEP WATER

Figure 4–2 Forced water sets for mink.

One mink I'd seen in the water headed not for shore but for one of these big trees. It crawled up onto it and then bounded along the top of it to shore. Moments later I saw it running out on another tree trunk.

The half-submerged tree I made my set on seemed a particularly good choice, because one day a mink had sprung onto it from shore and then run toward the end and crouched there as I glided by in the canoe. I've long admired mink and this was a big one. Now that its fur was prime, I hoped to catch it.

I cut a wide notch in the trunk and set the trap in it. I used a heavy staple to attach the trap chain to the underside of the tree and covered the trap lightly with dry moss.

I quit early that day and after canoeing back to the road where my truck was parked, I drove to our new campsite. This was about ten miles from where we were camped before and in a good deer hunting area. Today was the opening of deer season and I'd been hearing shots off and on all day. Aside from a two-year stint in the army, this was the first time I'd missed a deer opening in almost 30 years.

I was determined not to miss it completely and after parking the truck by our campsite, I headed for a tree stand I'd built a couple of weeks before. The stand gave me a good view of one end of a wild hay field. I'd killed a six-point buck here the year before. Now it felt good to sit and relax. Trapping is hard work.

I let my mind wander and thought back to the last night we spent at the river campsite before moving to this new location. I had put in a full day and checked every trap on my line, and I'd caught nothing. At that I'd had two traps stolen.

I wasn't very cheerful when I greeted Dave that night and said, "My only excitement today was finding two traps have been stolen."

"Oh no," Dave said. "I lost one, too."

"It's hard to make a profit at this rate," I complained. "Not that I expected to make a lot of money, but I would like to be able to cover the costs of gas and upkeep on the truck, not to mention the new traps and other equipment. I take it you didn't do any good either?"

"It was pretty slow," Dave said, as he stepped behind the tent and reached for something on the ground, "All I caught were these two."

Dave held up two big raccoons that we later weighed at 21 and 22 pounds.

"Oh, my gosh!" I exclaimed. "Where did you get them?"

Dave grinned and said, "I caught the one upstream from camp in the hollow tree, the same place I had one stolen. The other I caught in a dirt-hole set in the big field downstream from camp. And would you believe it? I ran into the scout troop I used to belong to. They're camped a couple of miles downstream. A guy I used to know in the troop got out of the Navy and is their Scoutmaster. It was fun talking with them. The kids were pretty excited about the raccoons I caught and asked a lot of questions about trapping."

My thoughts returned to the present, and to the field I was watching for deer. Dave, I knew, was also watching for deer, probably in the woods below camp. Both of us were so involved in trapping that we didn't have our usual enthusiasm for deer hunting. But I could feel some of that excitement returning as I pictured in my mind a big buck stepping into view.

Finally it grew dark and I headed out to our campsite. Our tent sat in a clearing that edged an old logging road. I could see smoke coming from the stovepipe and knew that Dave had already returned. I looked forward to talking over the day's events and soaking up the warmth of the fire. As I approached the tent, I wondered if Dave would have any more surprises.

"Any deer hidden behind the tent?" I asked.

"No, but it looks as though you did all right."

I'd almost forgotten the raccoon I'd caught that day on the small river and had left in the back of the truck. It was an immense female that weighed over 30 pounds. Later in the evening, I asked Dave what his plans were for the next day, "Are you planning to hunt deer?"

"No," Dave replied, "I want to go back to the river tomorrow and make some sets for mink and muskrat. I know of a couple sure-fire sets for both."

High-water den set

Dave knew of two muskrat dens above the waterline. The muskrats probably dug them when the river was high for so long. It looked as though they were still using them because there was a trail leading out of the water to each, although they wouldn't be able to use them once the river froze. They certainly weren't safe places for a muskrat to be, and Dave was sure that every mink that came by investigated those dens. Dave planned to set leg-hold traps in the water and killer traps in the den entrances.

Retreiving our river traps

We worked hard at setting traps during the next few days and then disaster struck—my truck broke down and the part needed was not available. It would be ten days before the truck was operating. In the meantime, it began to snow and the weather turned cold. In fact, a record for cold temperatures was set that winter. We managed to check our traps using my wife's car, but many days she needed it. Besides, it was becoming imperative that we pull our traps for the two river locations before the rivers froze. We needed the truck for pulling the boat and hauling the canoe.

Finally, the truck was fixed and Dave would be able to pull his traps on the big river while I canoed the small river to pull those we had set there. Heavy ice was already forming on both rivers and was worse on the small stream I had to navigate by canoe. We both should have gone in the

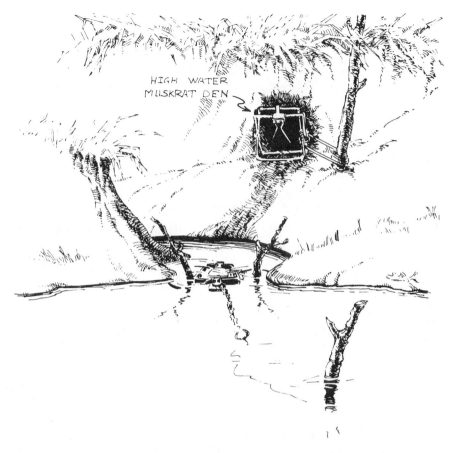

HIGH WATER
MUSKRAT DEN

Figure 4–3 Mink and muskrat sets.

canoe that day, but I insisted that I could handle it and Dave should get his traps pulled on the big river before that got any worse.

The major problem for me, at first, was getting close enough to shore to reach the traps. Anywhere from three to ten feet of ice edged the shoreline. There was much snow. By paddling furiously I could force the canoe's bow onto the ice, but in order to get out of the canoe I had to move to the front. The shifting of my weight would send the canoe sliding backward into open water.

Finally I looked first for good locations to beach the canoe and then, after beaching it, I'd walk to a set. Every set was frozen over and had to be chopped loose. The water level had risen nine inches before freezing and precluded any chance I would have a good catch. A couple of

61

muskrats had been caught before the water rose, however, and I held out hope I might catch a mink.

The ice grew worse. A bend in the river was frozen completely across. I could see another lane of open water beyond, and I was determined to reach it. By paddling furiously, and after many attempts, I got the canoe up onto the ice. Now, if I could slide it across the ice. . . .

Kneeling in the canoe, I put one leg over the side and pushed. It didn't budge. I shifted more of my weight to the ice. This time I made some headway, but I grew impatient. Finally I was walking bent over with both feet on the ice and my hands on the sides of the canoe. Now the canoe moved easily, but the lane of open water was getting close. Suddenly, the ice shattered and I plunged into the river. I was up to my hip pocket in water, and the canoe was taking in water and threatening to tip. Somehow, I managed to get one leg in it and, lunging desperately, I fell into the canoe. I paddled and fought my way to open water and then struggled for another ten minutes to reach shore.

Quickly I removed my knee-high rubber boots and the two pair of wool socks I was wearing. I wrung every drop of icy river water from the socks and hastily returned them to my feet. I slipped on my boots. It seemed a crazy thing to do, but I was going to keep going. I had more traps to retrieve.

After a seemingly interminable time only two traps remained to be retrieved, but the river was frozen almost solid. I'd fallen through twice more and twice more had stopped to wring the water out of my socks. I was chilled and operating on sheer will. I hardly dared to stop.

I began running through the snow, following the river, cutting cross-country where it made sharp bends, and looking frantically for those last two sets. Finally I saw an aspen stake sticking out of the ice where I'd set a Conibear trap in an underwater den entrance. Quickly I cut through the ice and withdrew the stake, trap, and what remained of a muskrat. A mink had eaten half of it.

I looked upstream to where my last trap was set on the tree trunk half-submerged in the river. I hurried to it and walked gingerly out onto it and put my foot where the trap should be under the snow. It was gone. Quickly I chopped a hole in the ice beside the tree and plunged my hand into the water and felt for the trap chain. I found it and lifted it, the trap, and a drowned mink to the surface. I wondered if it was the same mink that had dined on my muskrat.

I hardly had time to admire it or feel elated. I ran wildly back to the canoe and only then did I realize how very late it was getting. I couldn't possibly get back to the bridge before dark, and what's more, I didn't

Figure 4–4 I had waited too long to hop back into my canoe, and plunged through
the ice up to my hips.

have the energy left. I knew that by walking overland in an easterly direction I would reach the road where my truck was parked. It probably was less than a quarter of a mile. Dave and I could come back another day and skid the canoe out on the snow. I shouldered my pack full of traps and headed for the road. The mink and two intact muskrats lay on top.

Luck was with me that day. A car came by as I stumbled out onto the roadway and stopped when I raised my thumb. It didn't take long to reach my truck. I thanked the driver for the ride and started the ten-mile drive to the access site on the river where I was to pick up Dave. My feet were numb, but I knew it wasn't serious. The car heater was going full blast. I just hoped that Dave had gotten his traps safely. The big river could be dangerous. I didn't breather easily until I pulled into the access site and saw him unloading the boat.

I was feeling pretty good about the mink and two muskrats I'd caught and was about to tell Dave the good news, when he unceremoniously heaved a fat raccoon on the bank, followed by two muskrats, and two mink. The kid had done it again.

"I caught the raccoon upstream from the access," Dave told me later. "I'd baited a hole in the riverbank with muskrat flesh and the raccoon had tumbled to it. All the other traps on this end of the line were empty except for the two Conibear traps, each of which held a muskrat.

"Downstream the first set held a skunk, not exactly what I was hoping for. The next set was a muskrat den above the water-line. [This highwater den set was described earlier.] I'd set a 110 Conibear trap in the entrance and a No. 1½ double coil-spring trap in the water where a trail led from the water's edge to the den. The trap in the water was still set, but the Conibear trap was out of sight in the den entrance. Pulling on the chain I brought out the trap and found myself holding a prime mink.

"The next set was only five yards to my right and facing an area of frozen backwater. It was a dry-land set made in another high-water muskrat den. I'd set a Conibear trap in the dark recesses of the tunnel. Now I saw tracks in the snow leading into the den. I raced to the set and without bothering to examine the tracks, pulled out the trap and another mink. This was a big male. The jaws of the Conibear trap had closed around its neck and shoulders, killing it instantly.

"The rest of my traps were empty, but I'd had all the excitement I could take in one day. I'm going to miss running the river route."

I noticed we were catching a predominance of male mink, which was in our favor. Males bring a higher price than the females; they are larger and their thicker hide holds the fur better and makes for longer-lasting fur coats. The two largest were caught in culverts. Culvert sets, such as

Figure 4–5 One of a number of large male mink we caught.

described in Chapter 3 tend to catch the big males that do a lot of traveling. When you trap deep in the woods, you more often take young mink and females that are living in a fairly limited area.

A few days later, while hiking through a swamp of cedar and spruce enroute to a secluded stretch of small creek where I had mink sets, I felt the thrill of spotting a bobcat track. I built a pine-bough cubby and baited it with the carcass of a raccoon that I'd planned to haul to the dump. Bobcat season would open December 1, and I wanted to keep the cat interested.

One day we found a small creek and the tracks of one or two mink in the snow. There were a couple spots of open water; otherwise, it was frozen. We made several sets using sardines as bait. We set the bait amid a tangle of cover that the mink had been going through. A few days later, it was obvious that a mink had approached one set to within three feet of a 110 Conibear trap, then backed off, obviously spooked. Dave and I had each set a trap at the same time at this location and we may have left a lot of scent. Either that or the Conibear trap spooked it. Everything is more difficult to trap when snow and cold set in. Tracks in the snow tell many stories and you can really see when animals are evading your sets.

The Conibear trap for muskrat

I've grown increasingly appreciative of the Conibear trap. While a muskrat may twist out of a leg-hold trap if they aren't set properly, they never get out of a Conibear trap. A simple animal, muskrats will walk through a fully exposed Conibear trap to reach a bait or simply get where they want to go. A friend of mine did a lot of open-water muskrat trapping that fall and used the Conibear trap almost exclusively. I asked Steve how he went about trapping the muskrats on lakes and marshes. I knew he would give sound advice. Steve catches a lot of muskrats, and he does so in heavily trapped, close-to-town lakes and marshes.

"There are hundreds of set locations," Steve said. "Sometimes I set Conibear traps in the trails and tunnels that muskrats make in the marsh vegetation—blind sets, the same as in trapping mink. I make a lot of baited sets by feed beds and the edges of muskrat houses. In the case of a muskrat house, I make a dent maybe four to six inches deep in the side of the house, put bait and lure in back, and the Conibear trap in front. At a feed bed, where muskrats gather to eat and you find fresh root and stem cuttings, I put a slice of apple on a stick. Just be sure the muskrat has to go through the trap to reach it.

"I use the Conibear trap inside muskrat houses and feeders, too. I feel around for an underwater tunnel leading to the outside and set the trap in the tunnel. This year it was illegal to trap within a muskrat house, but you could trap within a feeder, or pushup as they are sometimes called.

"The difference between a muskrat house and a feeder, aside from the house usually being larger, is the muskrat house is built in summer from

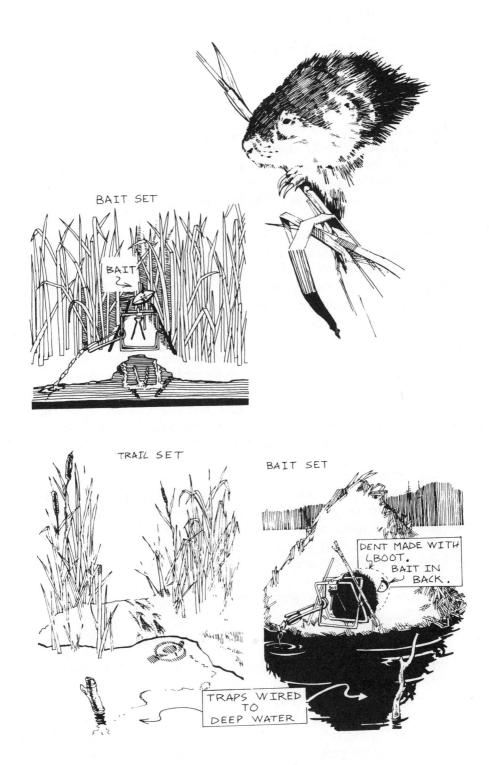

BAIT SET

BAIT

TRAIL SET

BAIT SET

DENT MADE WITH
BOOT.
BAIT IN
BACK.

TRAPS WIRED
TO
DEEP WATER

Figure 4–6 Several muskrat sets.

67

the lake bottom on up. It is made of cattails, bulrushes, and other wide-bladed grasses. The feeder, or pushup, is built *after* freeze-up on *top* of the ice. The muskrat has to gnaw a hole in the ice to do it. It is made of roots and other things the muskrat dredges up from the bottom. It may be darker and a little lumpier in appearance than a house."

Viewed from above the ice, it is very hard to tell the difference between a muskrat house and a feeder. I asked our local game law enforcement people about this and they admitted they find it difficult to tell the difference.

A feeder is simply a place where the muskrat can come up for a breath of air and feed on some delicacy it has found. It can also feed in its house, but a muskrat house also contains its bed. The muskrat's bed is usually a shallow depression in a dry spot in the house. In a house actively being used, this bed will be warm to the touch.

I notice that in this year's trapping regulations it is also illegal to trap in feeder, probably because trappers and game officials alike have trouble differentiating between the two. In years when muskrat numbers are plentiful, it is usually permissible to trap in both houses and feeders.

Steve continued. "I'm always on the lookout for underwater entrances to bank dens. They're hard to spot but are sure-fire sets. Often overlooked are beaver ponds. We've had midwinter beaver seasons the last couple of years and I always make a few baited sets for muskrat if I find open water."

"Incidentally, it pays to use lure along with baited sets. Usually food lure, but muskrat gland lure is good and so is oil of anise. You can buy that at the drugstore. Seems like anything sweet smelling appeals to them. I usually use a slice of apple for bait. But you know, late in the season they start getting a little leary of bait. Then I use lure only."

I thought of how Steve's advice on trapping muskrat compared with what we were experiencing trapping mink. We planned to concentrate more on muskrat after the lakes and marshes froze.

The Conibear trap for mink

When trapping mink, the Conibear trap should first be boiled in logwood dye and be free of all but a wood odor. It should then be set in such a way that its shape and outline are not clearly defined. The ideal set would be a tunnel through thick grass and weeds just wide enough and high enough to fit the trap and partially obscure the jaws. I don't think that mink can recognize a trap as such, but the shape of the trap is not natural with the surroundings.

Figure 4–7 The mud was plastered with mink tracks by the base of this tree, but the 110 Conibear trap is too exposed. The set did not produce.

Of course, a dry-land set should never be made with one of the killer traps in any place where a domestic animal could get into it. In many states, the 330-size killer trap, usually recommended for beaver, is illegal to use on dry land.

The Conibear trap works beautifully in water sets, particularly in a narrow space between exposed tree roots and bank. The set is made in a few inches of water with the lower jaws of the trap below the surface.

In a dry-land set, I prefer to have the lower jaws of the trap slightly off the ground if the ground is damp because of the possibility of their freezing in place. Sometimes I lay a couple of dry twigs under them. And I'm fussy about the trap setting solidly. A delicately balanced Conibear trap could be knocked over before the animal is in it. I hold it upright by pushing a stick into the ground at an angle near one side so the top of the stick rests between the upper jaws. Two sticks can be used, one on each side. (See the drawings of muskrat sets in Figure 4-6.) Then I put a stake either through the end of the spring or the end of the trap chain.

The most important thing is that the trap sets in such a way that the mink has no choice but to go through it. The mink may not be disturbed by the trap, but if there is a way to go around, it is very likely to choose that route. Obviously you cannot prevent this entirely unless you set the trap within the entrance to a narrow hole or tunnel, but you can block the immediate avenues of detour. I used to be wary of using guide sticks. They looked phony and unnatural to me, but I finally decided that they don't bother a mink one bit. Don't hesitate to use them.

I remember two instances that winter when the Conibear trap was uniquely useful in trapping mink in snow. In both cases I'd found that a mink was popping in and out of holes that went straight down into openings in a beaver dam. Everything was covered with a heavy blanket of snow. The holes the mink were using were not much bigger around than the mink and, as I've already said, dropped straight down.

In each case, I lay a Conibear trap on its side directly over the hole. By pushing the trap gently into the soft, fluffly snow, it all but disappeared. It did disappear when I smoothed over the surface. All I, or a mink, could see of it were the trigger wires in the hole. Both traps remained in good working condition because of continuous sub-zero temperatures. Once it started thawing during the day and freezing at night, however, they were useless.

According to the notes I kept during our four months of trapping, I found mink heaven on November 25. I'd walked out into a marshy area I'd found in the summer. It was a time of high water when I first discovered it and I couldn't tell much at the time except that there was a lot of marsh and perhaps some open water in the middle. Now I walked out on the frozen surface and found muskrat houses and feeders. But the most interesting discovery was some pockets of open water. Mink had been entering and exiting those pockets of open water leaving beaten trails in the snow. Just beyond was a creek and more open water could be seen.

It was late afternoon when I found this spot and I was worn out from a full day of checking traps. At that the weather was getting colder by the hour. But now I felt a surge of enthusiasm. I had a half dozen leg-hold traps in my pack and planned to set them in the water where the mink had been crawling out onto the snow.

It was risky getting near the open water which, I suspected, was caused by springs, but I was wearing hip boots and hoped the water was not deep. It was. At least, it was too deep to set a trap where the mink had been coming out of the water. So I dredged handfuls of vegetation from the bottom and piled it below the surface where I wanted to set a trap. I was able to build a pile to within two inches of the surface in two spots and set a trap on each pile. How could I miss?

I found out a few days later. Dave and I returned and found every set frozen over. There was still some open water beyond where the traps were set, so I chopped away the newly formed ice. It would probably freeze again that night, but I remembered what Charlie Mechley had told me about chopping away the ice from a set and sometimes catching a mink in it during those few hours before ice reformed.

Muskrat house and feeder sets

We set traps for muskrat in every feeder we could find. We did this by chopping a hole in the side of the feeder and setting the frozen chunks to one side. Then we dug out several handfuls of wet vegetation and feed from the inside and put this in another pile. Next we set a leg-hold trap inside the feeder where we determined the muskrats were sitting while they fed. In some feeders there was only enough room to squeeze a trap inside and no choice to set it wherever it fit.

We attached two feet of soft, flexible wire to each trap chain and coiled this inside with the trap. The other end of the wire was twisted on to a sapling propped on the outside of the feeder. We put the frozen chunks we'd chopped loose back into place and plastered the wet vegetation we'd kept separate over the frozen chunks. The wet vegetation would quickly freeze and seal the feeder and prevent the water inside from freezing. When a muskrat was caught, the length of soft wire would allow it to dive into its underwater tunnel where it would then drown. The procedure for trapping in a muskrat house is the same, although in a house I like to set the trap in the muskrat's nest. You don't find a dry nest in a feeder.

We caught muskrats, but the bitterly cold weather continued to freeze the open-water mink sets. Finally those pockets of open water were frozen solid. There was some open water below an old beaver dam on the creek, but another trapper had already set traps there and I didn't want to crowd him. Too many trappers in one area only spoils it for everyone, especially when you are trapping the slyer animals.

71

CHILLY WORK, CHECKING MUSKRAT FEEDERS

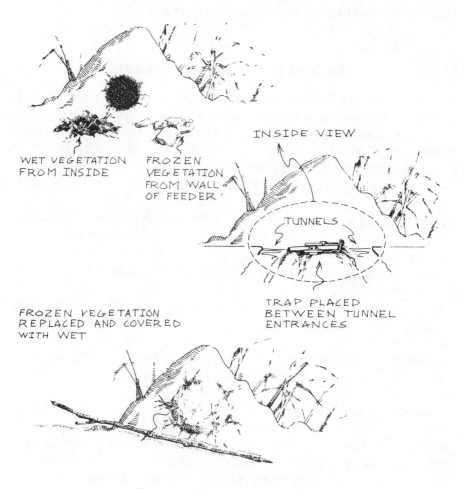

WET VEGETATION
FROM INSIDE

FROZEN
VEGETATION
FROM WALL
OF FEEDER

INSIDE VIEW

TUNNELS

TRAP PLACED
BETWEEN TUNNEL
ENTRANCES

FROZEN VEGETATION
REPLACED AND COVERED
WITH WET

Figure 4–8 Feeder set for muskrat.

72

Figure 4–9 Dave removes a muskrat from a feeder, or pushup.

Besides, by this time I was paranoid about where I set my traps. We'd had 20 traps and numerous animals stolen and would lose even more before the season was over. Fellow trappers are the last on my list of suspects. I remember one day when Dave and I walked along a small creek and sighted a mink in a leg-hold trap. The mink was dead. We paused to admire it and probably felt a twinge of envy, but the thought of stealing the animal or trap never entered our minds. I think most trappers have this same respect for one another.

In our part of the country, most traps are stolen by weekend duck, deer, and grouse hunters. They have no earthly use for the traps and probably pick them up as souvenirs. What bothers me most are the deliberate trap thieves who make a point of looking for traps.

One day we set five traps in feeders on a small pond near road side. We caught three muskrats the first day. The next day we found that all five traps had been stolen. The tracks in the snow indicated that someone had come during the middle of the night and followed our route in the moonlit snow. It was disheartening to see the feeders torn open and left that way to freeze.

Another time I had three snares set within 75 yards of a road being crossed by a coyote. One day I noticed that a car had stopped about 50 yards from where I normally walked into the woods. The car's occupant had walked into the woods and then turned and walked parallel with the road until he reached my snowshoe trail that led to my three snares. The first snare had held a coyote, and this person had taken it. That coyote was worth a minimum of $75. What is worse, I suspect the individual who took it was a trapper. That really hurt.

Stepping sticks

We learned the value of using a stepping stick with our mink sets that winter. The season on mink continued through the month of December, and while we occasionally were able to make sets in open water, most of our trapping was done in snow on the frozen surfaces of lakes and streams. Aside from the usual difficulties of keeping our traps functioning, we had to deal with the mink's peculiar hopping gait. Their hind feet land approximately in the same tracks as their front feet, with 18 inches or more space between the tracks. In order to get the mink to step on our trap, we used a stepping stick.

A stepping stick for mink must be very skinny. I used a blade of timothy hay or a twig no greater than one-eighth inch in diameter. This was laid

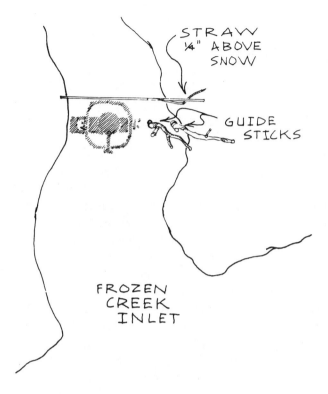

Figure 4–10 Straw used for a stepping stick.

crosswise directly in front of the trap and about half an inch above the ground, snow, and occasionally water. It wasn't difficult to find some way to prop it off the surface.

While hopping toward one of our traps, the mink would see the stepping stick and, surprisingly, this would break its stride, it would then step over the stick and into the trap. Even when it came from the other direction, it would break stride and slow to a walk in order to step over the stick, which would usually land it in our trap. It is important to keep the stepping stick for mink to the size of a straw or blade of grass so the mink doesn't step on the stick and then, possibly, step over the trap.

This is not normally a problem in water because mink will walk rather than hop while in the water. Even so, I sometimes use a stepping stick in water sets, especially very shallow water. A culvert may have an inch of water running through it, but mink often hop while running through a trickle of water in a pipe.

You can break the stride of a fox, coyote, or wolf the same way. For these larger animals, use a stepping stick around pencil thickness and prop it up a little higher off the ground.

Dave took an artist's job with our area's Department of Natural Resources on December 1 and from then on joined me on weekends only. I kept him informed of happenings on the line and in particular the frustrations of trapping mink in snow.

There was the time I made three sets in a row in culverts under a road that parallels the river. I could see by its tracks in the snow that a mink had been following the river and running on the frozen surfaces of every little tributary and through these culverts. I figured the mink would return in five or six days. It did. By then, however, there had been more snowfall and the county snowplow had been down the road and sent a geyser of snow into the ditches and buried every trap.

One weekend Dave and I each set traps where fresh mink tracks followed the frozen surface of a ditch. Five days later the mink returned and stepped one-half inch from the pan of one of Dave's traps and directly onto one of mine. But the trigger mechanism was stiff and the mink's light step failed to trip it. It pays to make every set in areas of constant shade. The afternoon sun, even in sub-zero temperatures, can moisten the snow's surface and this freezes hard after sundown.

One day I found a trickle of open water below a beaver dam. It was about one foot wide and one inch deep. I could see where a mink was running through the snow and then stepping into the open water and following it to the bottom of the dam. I set two traps side by side in the water. I wanted to get that mink. But when I checked the set I found the water level had dropped and the trickle gone dry—the two traps were frozen in the mud.

There was one consolation in that I had little competition with other trappers. Most prefer to do their mink trapping during the early days of fall. By this time I was concentrating on putting out snares for coyote, but when I found mink tracks in the snow I never hesitated to make sets for the animal. They are thickly furred at this time and bring top prices. It is a challenge I find hard to resist.

5

Coyote, Bobcat, and Fisher

Some trappers consider the coyote to be the most difficult of all North American animals to trap. A timber wolf, they say, will walk into a suspicious situation and depend on its brute strength to get it out of trouble. The coyote takes no chances. Well, I've never had the opportunity to trap timber wolves, but I can attest to the trap-wise nature of the coyote. I set my first trap for coyote on October 21.

Everything looked bright for those early days. I'd dug and prebaited dirt-hole sets and coyotes were visiting and taking the bait at a half-dozen or more locations. In some locations I had two or three holes dug and the visiting coyote would dig at every one. Finding their tracks in the sifted dirt in front of the holes was electrifying.

I'd had considerable experience snaring coyotes, but had never pursued them with leg-hold traps, and what I thought would be a good start turned sour. When I set traps, the coyotes stopped coming.

I had only nine days of trapping time before the opening of deer season when I planned to pull the traps. I would set them again after the 200,000 to 300,000 hunters went home. I knew that during the deep winter it took a coyote nine to ten days to complete its hunting route and return to any one spot a second time, but in the early fall there is an abundance of food and they will return more often. They also hunt mice in open fields then and many of my sets were in hay and clover fields, although I also had sets in clearings that edged on logging trails. Later in the winter they would stay more in deep forest and live along the edges of cedar swamps and other deer-wintering areas.

Dave was involved in running the river trapline at this time but planned to join me later in the winter in setting snares for coyote.

It may seem strange to the uninitiated that I had difficulty with early fall coyote trapping. I think old timers will understand. The problem, I suspect, was foreign odor on my equipment. It could have been the wire I used to attach trap chains to trap stakes. This should have been boiled in logwood dye along with my traps. Never underestimate a coyote's nose—you're in trouble if you do. For a while there I was beginning to wonder if it wouldn't help if I jumped in a pot of logwood dye, too.

When I pulled my traps nine days later I hadn't taken a single coyote. I wondered if I shouldn't forget about them until the time of deep snow when I would pursue them with the familiar snare. But I was intrigued. I vowed to reboil everything. I put traps, stakes, lashing wire, and anything else I could think of into a boiling solution of logwood dye. I also bought more of the coyote urine I'd used before the season. I had run out of that particular supplier's brand and bought another brand locally to use during the season. I never did like the odor of the urine I bought locally— it smelled suspiciously like a barnyard. That too may have contributed to my early-season coyote problems. I was suspicious as well of the plastic sandwich bags I was using for trap covers. I wondered if they didn't emit some odor.

I was so busy at this time running traps for fox and raccoon that I had to do all this boiling and dyeing of traps and other gear at night. But I was enjoying every minute of it. I'd already lost ten pounds and would lose ten more. I hadn't felt so good in years.

Buried skunk sets

One of the best tips I got from Charlie Mechley was to use the all but worthless skunks that got into my traps for coyote bait. The idea is to bury the skunk except for the tip of its tail which acts as a flasher, attracting a coyote should it pass upwind of the set. Buried skunks are especially good for winter trapping because the odor (the more odor the better) seeps through the ground and is detectable all winter. Should I manage to kill a skunk without its releasing its vile smelling defense weapon, it was suggested that I deliberately pierce the animals scent sacks.

The first skunk I buried right on the spot. I'd caught it in a dirt-hole set that was actually an old animal den. I'd tossed bait into it and was attracting coyote before season, but my first catch was a skunk. After shooting it, I pushed it down into the hole and buried all but the tip of its tail. I pulled the trap because I wanted to clean it. Considerable blood had attached to it when I shot the skunk. I planned to set a clean trap here immediately after the deer season. Four days later a coyote came by, dug up the skunk, and ate half of it.

After deer season I shoved what remained of the skunk into the hole and buried it a second time. I set two No. 3 Oneida jump traps in the surface soil, lightly covering each with a quarter-inch of dirt. Each trap was wired to a separate hardwood drag, a three-foot length of three- to four-inch-thick aspen. Before attaching the wire I determined the balance point and cut a groove for the wire. When a coyote pulled it, I wanted the drag to pull crosswise. If you attach the wire too close to either end, the drag will pull end first and the coyote may travel a long distance before tangling. Some trappers prefer to use a metal, two-pronged grapple for a drag. (For details, see Chapter 12.)

Figure 5–1 Buried skunk set for coyote.

There was snow on the ground and I concealed the drags, trap chains, and wire in it. If there had not been snow, I would have cut a shallow trench with my hatchet to conceal each drag and made a cut in the ground in which to press the wire and trap chain. I used drags rather than stakes because the soil was loose from burying the skunk, and a stake might pull free. Besides, with two traps and each trap wired to a separate drag, it was possible to make a double catch. I smoothed the dirt that covered the traps using a pine bough. (This was dry dirt that I'd carried in.) Then I sprinkled coyote urine over the area of sifted dirt and concealed traps and smoothed the disturbed snow with the pine bough.

I caught my first coyote in this set. It stepped into both traps and did not get far before tangling in underbrush. Despite its predicament, this small version of a wolf looked resplendent in its grizzled-grey coat, flecked with splashes of silver and black. It seemed to emanate a calm intelligence. Finding that coyote waiting for me after so much trial and error was one of the high points of a trapline I'll long remember.

Dirt-hole sets

The dirt-hole set is still the top producer for coyote as it is for fox, and I continued using it after snowfall; but snow, and we got more and more of it, is a complicating element.

Fall and early winter are the best times to trap coyotes in dirt-hole sets. The steps for making one are essentially the same as for building one for fox, as described in Chapter 3. Here's how to build one from scratch:

1. Pick a location.
2. Choose a back-stop.
3. Remove sod.
4. Dig the hole.
5. Dig the trap bed.
6. Pound in the trap stake.
7. Set the trap.
8. Change gloves.
9. Add bait and lure.
10. Change gloves.
11. Retrieve equipment.
12. Brush out tracks.
13. Add coyote urine.

Now let's take them one at a time:

COYOTE, BOBCAT, AND FISHER

1. Pick a location. Sometimes this is very easy. One day while grouse hunting I saw a young coyote hunting mice in a field of clover. There wasn't a doubt in my mind that I'd be making dirt-hole set in that field, probably 20 to 50 feet from the woods that bordered one edge. When a farmer friend told me he heard coyotes howling almost every night near his place, I had another potential spot for the dirt-hole set.

Mostly I selected spots that looked good to me, such as an area of open grass where a homestead once stood and small clearings along logging trails in country that I knew to contain coyote or where someone told me there were coyotes. I looked for wild plum thickets; coyotes are crazy about wild plums. I looked for any kind of clearing in otherwise forested terrain, and I looked for coyote tracks and droppings. The smartest thing I did, however, was to do the preliminary digging and baiting before season. This enabled me to know if a spot was really good or just looked good.

2. Choose a back-stop. This can be a tuft of grass, a low rock, a rotting log, a slight embankment, or almost anything that will discourage the coyote from approaching your set from behind instead of in front where the trap is. Don't feel that a set cannot be made because there is no back-stop. For one thing, you can carry a rock or whatever to the spot where you want to make the set. Just be certain that the backing is no more than one foot high. The coyote must be able to see over and around it. After all, it thinks it is stealing the food cache of another animal and, like a trap thief, it is very nervous about getting caught.

Quite frankly, I made a lot of dirt-hole sets with little or no back-stop. The triangular shape of the set, with the bait hole in one corner of the triangle, leads the animal into the trap.

3. Remove sod. Cut out a triangular patch of sod about one foot on each side, with one corner of the triangle against the back-stop. You could make the set more noticeable by cutting a larger piece of sod, but this size is adequate. If the sod is very tough it may be difficult to cut it out with a conventional dirt-hole digging tool. We frequently used a garden spade. Incidentally, this set does work well in clay soil, unless you want to carry in dirt to cover your trap with. At that, such dirt can be suspicious to an older, educated coyote.

I always looked for patches of light, sandy soil. I remember reading of a coyote trapper in Michigan who made all his sets in sand dunes along Lake Michigan. We should all be so lucky. In pure sand or where there is little to no sod, it is only necessary to loosen the soil and discard any rocks or tufts of root.

Figure 5–2 It wasn't necessary to remove sod in digging a dirt-hole set in this sandy location.

All sod that is removed should be shaken over the excavated triangle to remove loose dirt, then thrown out of sight or carried away and discarded.

4. Dig the hole. In the corner by the back-stop, dig the bait hole about four to six inches wide by eight inches deep at a 45-degree angle under the back-stop. Put this dirt in your sifter.

5. Dig the trap bed. Directly in front of the bait hole, dig a trap bed that will allow the trap dog, or trigger mechanism, to sit one inch from the edge of the hole. The bed should be deep enough so the trap, when covered with dirt, will be level with, or slightly below the level of, the surrounding dirt. Put the dirt from the bed in your sifter.

6. Pound in the trap stake. Despite their being powerful animals, you can hold coyote with a stake providing the chain is wired or otherwise clamped or bolted to the stake close to the trap about the fourth or fifth chain link from the trap. The stake for coyote should be 15 to 18 inches long. Pound the stake in the center of the trap bed until it is completely out of sight.

Some trappers, as an added precaution, will have a two-pronged grapple attached to the end of the trap chain and buried several inches under the trap. Be sure the steel grapple has been boiled in logwood dye.

7. Set the trap. Cock the trap and adjust the trap pan to a hair trigger. Set the trap firmly in the trap bed and snuggle it down into the loose dirt. The idea is to have the trap firmly in place so that it will not rock should a coyote step on the edge of a jaw instead of the trap pan. Lift the loose jaw, the one opposite of the trigger mechanism, and insert your wax paper or canvas trap cover under the jaw and over the trap pan with the corners under the other jaw. I use a stick to poke the cover under the other jaw. Lower the loose jaw. Now pick up your sifter and sift dirt over the trap until it is barely covered. A pyramid shaped pile may develop over the trap pan. This can be leveled with the edge of your hatchet blade. Sift a little dirt over the entire triangle.

8. Change gloves. Next, you should put on the pair of gloves that you wear solely for handling bait and gland lure. Eventually, no matter how careful you are, you're going to spill a little lure or juice from the bait onto your gloves. This is no problem as long as you wear these gloves solely for handling bait and lure. I like to pin mine to the outside of my pack sack when I'm not using them. I don't want them near the rest of my equipment.

9. Add bait and lure. A piece of stiff wire works well for spearing a chunk of bait from the bait jar. For a while I used a fondue fork. Whatever you use, it, as well as the bait, lure, and the gloves you now have on, must be kept separate from the rest of your gear.

Being careful not to spill any juice over the trap, drop the bait into the hole. Some trappers like to cover this bait lightly with dirt. We did this some of the time, but I'm not sure that it makes a bit of difference. Next, dip a two-inch twig into your bottle of gland lure and drop it into the bait hole.

10. Change gloves. Remove the gloves you wear for handling bait and lure. Put on the pair reserved for handling traps and other equipment.

11. Retrieve equipment. This may seem obvious, but it is very easy to walk away and leave some piece of equipment at the set location. Make sure that everything is safely stored away in your pack.

12. Brush out tracks. I frequently use my digging tool to straighten the grass where I've been standing. You might want to carry a pine bough or

Figure 5–3 Here I complete a set by sifting dirt over the trap. The bait jar seen here should have been kept in my pack instead of on the ground where it could add unwanted odor to the set.

Figure 5–4 Here a twig is dipped into a bottle of gland lure. The twig is then deposited in the bottom of the dirt hole.

clump of pine boughs tied together. Some trappers will carry a broom stub. If there is snow, I like to smooth over my tracks for several yards.

13. Add coyote urine. The final touch, as you are backing away from the set, is to sprinkle coyote urine over the dirt where your trap is set and the ground where you've been standing. It does no harm if this urine gets on the gloves you wear for handling traps and equipment; in fact, it's a good idea to put some on purposely. It is a very natural odor and calms a suspicious animal. It thinks another of its kind has been there before it. It is standard procedure to sprinkle a little of this urine on the sole of your rubber boots.

Figure 5–5 A coyote is investigating a dirt-hole set.

When making sets for coyote in locations that I believed might produce red fox as well, I used red fox urine instead of coyote urine at the set, the idea being a coyote will not hesitate to steal from a fox's food cache. On the other hand, the fox is so frightened of a coyote that it may hesitate to approach a set where it believes a coyote has been. How true this is it's hard to say. The gland lure I used was made with glands from fox, coyote, wolf, wildcats, and muskrat, yet it lured all of them, not to mention raccoon and skunk. Urine is more of an immediate thing, however, and an animal approaching the set may believe that the animal that left its calling card is near at hand.

Incidentally, it's hard to beat rubber boots when making the dirt-hole and other sets for coyote. I slosh mine periodically in the nearest pond or creek. Also, if wearing cotton or canvas gloves for general handling of traps and equipment, I sometimes grasp the boughs of pine trees as I walk by. The odor of pine is a natural one in my area and is not likely to arouse suspicion in trap-wise animals.

It's not a bad idea to use a ground cloth when making sets. This is a fairly heavy piece of canvas, say two feet square. Put it on the ground at the set location and stand or kneel on it while making the set. Just be sure to have the same side up at every set, fold it with the "down" side in, and store it carefully with your gear so it does not absorb unwanted odors.

Fine-tuning your traps

Imagine how convenient it would be to cock a trap and have it set automatically to a hair trigger with the pan level and without any adjusting on your part. In the case of coyote trapping, you'd want a trap pan that requires two pounds of pressure to trip the trap, for fox, only about one-half to one pound of pressure.

You can modify any leg-hold trap to have an automatic hair trigger and a trap pan that sets level with the trap jaws. Start by filing the end of the trap trigger to a 45-degree angle. The angle should be on the under side of the trigger. This leaves a sharp, very abrupt edge to fit into the receiver. The notch in the receiver should be filed down so the edge of the trigger will barely fit.

At this point you will have a trap pan that sticks far too high in the air when the trap is set. What remains is to make modifications that will level the pan to where you want it. Two modifications are needed: bending the trap trigger to a shallow V-shape and bending inward that part of the framework that holds the trigger. Experiment with one of your traps and see how you like it. You'll need a metal file, a hammer, and a vise.

Any of the sly canines will place their feet lightly in a suspicious situation. If a trap springs too easily all you may catch is a toenail. Ideally, you want the trap to spring shut when the animal has its full weight on it. In the case of coyote, about two pounds of pressure to trip the hair trigger would be about right. That will insure a high catch on the animal's foot.

To modify pan tension, you must use traps that come with adjustable trap pans, such as the No. 2 and 3 Victor coil-spring traps. The adjustment is a nut and bolt. Increase pan tension by tightening the bolt and decrease by loosening the bolt. In adjusting the pan to take two pounds of pressure, most trappers go by feel. They tighten the bolt, cock the trap, and then trip the trap by inserting their thumb under the trap jaw and pressing down on the pan. If it feels like it takes about two pounds of

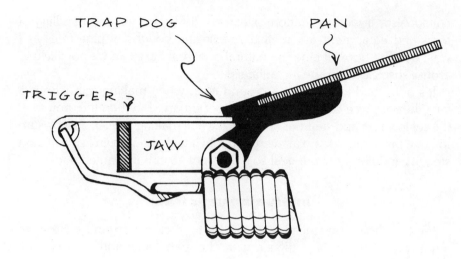

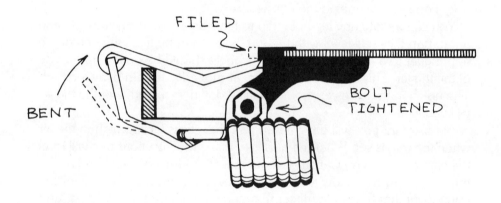

Figure 5–6 Fine-tuning a trap.

pressure to trip it, they are satisfied. If you wanted to be more exact, you could use a two-pound weight on the trap pan. Start with a lot of tension on the bolt and then loosen it until the weight trips the trap.

Bobcat and fisher

On December 1 the season opened for bobcat and fisher. There were no fisher within the area I was trapping, but I hoped to locate and trap a couple by driving further north where the country is more heavily forested. There were a few bobcat around, say five or six, and I built two cubby sets on opening day and set traps at a couple of others that I had built before the season. These had been built near where I'd seen cat tracks.

I hoped to find greater populations of bobcat when I drove north in search of fisher. There was a limit on both animals—a trapper could take three fisher and six bobcat. Every animal had to be tagged and inspected by a conservation officer.

I have a tendency to lump bobcat and fisher together. While they are completely different animals, the problems involved in trapping them and the methods used are very similar. For example, neither animal knows where it's going to be from one day to the next. While they seem to follow a hunting route, they do not show the tendency of the wild canines to return and follow the same trails each time. They will return to a certain area but rarely cross a logging trail in the same spot. Sometimes they do, but they are so erratic and unpredictable that one never knows. At that it takes them three weeks or more to complete their hunting route.

Figure 5–7 Fisher.

A MODERN TRAPLINE

It is fortunate for their survival that they are so unpredictable, because neither animal is trap-wise. If you can find where a bobcat or fisher is feeding on a deer carcass or a large bait of any kind, it is relatively easy to catch the animal. Both will holeup near the free meal and not leave the area until they have eaten every scrap.

Because they were scarce in the country I was trapping and such fascinating animals, the sight of a bobcat track always got my blood up. I remember one brutally long hike I made down an old logging trail. The snow was deep and I was wearing snowshoes. In my pack I carried snares to set in coyote trails and I had two No. 3 jump traps. I was looking for coyote tracks and setting the snares for them whenever I found a track. By the time I headed out to the road, following my own snowshoe trail back, it was very late, almost dusk.

Suddenly I stopped. An animal had crossed the tracks I made less than an hour before. And there was blood, meaning the animal had crossed my trail carrying something it had killed in its mouth. Part of the kill was dragging in the snow and leaving a trail of blood.

The snow was soft and fluffy, and it was difficult to identify the animal's track. I followed the tracks into the trees and, under the protective boughs of a spruce tree where the snow was shallow, I say they were that of a large bobcat. Moments later I found the remains of a snowshoe rabbit. There wasn't much.

I backtracked the bobcat and a few yards on the other side of the logging trail found where it had made the kill. I went back and stuffed what remained of that rabbit into the base of a hollow stump and set a trap in front. I'd shot a rabbit earlier and I hung that from a tree limb directly over the trap and about five to six feet above it. There was no reason for the cat to return to the kill, so I wanted to attract its attention if it came this way again. Such tactics as hanging a bait over a trap would scare the socks off a coyote but you have to be obvious with bobcat. They have poor noses and sometimes seem blind as well.

Later in the week I hung a partridge wing above the logging trail and even tied tin pie plates by light thread from nearby trees. The slightest breeze would cause them to spin. They shimmered and sparkled in the moonlight. Cats really are curious and I hoped these tactics would lure one close enough to my set to see or smell it. I'd never seen a bobcat track in this area of woodlands before and was pretty excited about it, but I never saw that cat's track again.

So it was doubly exciting for me when I found that a bobcat in another area had found the raccoon carcass I'd put out for bait. At first I had put the carcass in the back of a three-sided cubby built along an old logging

Figure 5–8 Close-up of a bobcat, one of the most interesting animals on our trapline.

trail, using pine boughs for a roof. Two traps guarded the entrance. The problem was that the cat, which on rare and unpredictable times crossed the trail, never noticed it. Finally I put the carcass out in front, in the center of the trail. I still had some scraps of bait in the cubby where the traps were set.

I hoped by putting the bait in the open that ravens would find it. Ravens will consume a lot of carrion and would make short work of the bait, but their raucous cries and the sight of them circling overhead might help the bobcat to find it. Finally, to aid the ravens even more, I carried the carcass to a high, open knoll. Still, it was another week before the ravens found it and a bobcat moved in.

I set two traps, one by the bait and the other in the trail the bobcat made in approaching the bait. I figured the latter set would be safe from a

Figure 5–9 Once this bobcat found the bait I'd put out, catching it was not difficult.

raven stepping into it. I made a depression in the snow for a trap bed. I had no trap covers and simply set the trap in the depression and brushed snow over it. You could still see the shape of the trap. That wouldn't bother the cat. Besides, it was snowing and the trap would be concealed by the new snow. The snow was dry and as long as the weather didn't warm, the trap would function. I caught the cat four days later. It was a young female, beautifully furred. I got a good price for it.

Cubby Sets

During the course of the winter I developed a favorite set for bobcat and fisher. The site for the set was determined by following a track, fresh or old, until I found where the animal had crossed an opening.

Figure 5–10 Cubby set for bobcat or fisher.

BEAVER CARCASS
BAIT

TRAPS WIRED
TO DRAG

Favorite locations were the frozen surfaces of beaver ponds and creeks. I would then place the skinned carcass of one of the beavers I'd trapped where ravens or crows would find it. I hoped their noisy cries would attract the bobcat or fisher. Other good baits include almost anything meaty. Porcupine, natural prey for the fisher, is excellent.

Next I would build a cubby nearby. Usually I would use the trunk of a spruce or balsam for the back of the cubby and pine boughs and dead sticks for the sides and roof. I put bait and lure in the back of the cubby. I used canned sardines with good results for both bobcat and fisher. I would set one or two traps in the entrance and wire them to a hardwood drag.

There are advantages to setting traps in a cubby instead of out by the big bait. For one thing, ravens and other birds of prey will not walk into an enclosure. They don't even care to land in heavy cover, so there is small chance of catching one in your trap. More important, you can make the set almost weatherproof and improve the chances of your trap working in adverse conditions. Just building the set under an evergreen helps.

I like to tramp down the snow where I'm going to build the cubby. Then, when I set a trap, I can usually scrape away a trap-size patch of snow right down to the bare ground, and the concealed trap will be level with the surrounding snow. Before setting the trap in this excavated spot I lay a piece of wax paper under it. Sometimes that is all I do, except for sprinkling dead pine needles on the trap pan and between the jaws. A light covering is all that is needed, especially with a blackened trap and if guide sticks and a small, pencil-thin stepping stick are used in front of the trap. For surer results in adverse weather, put a second piece of wax paper under the trap jaws and over the pan. Be sure to use only a smattering of pine needles or other covering. The tiniest twig caught near one end of the jaws will prevent their closing properly.

A word of warning: Don't use any green wood (except pine boughs) in building the cubby. Use dead limbs and branches. Green aspen branches, for instance, are food to snowshoe rabbits and will have them flocking into your cubby and traps.

Once a bobcat or fisher is lured to the large bait, you can depend on its finding the nearby cubby and investigating the interesting smells inside.

Trail sets

Coyote, bobcat, and fisher can all be caught in trail sets such as those described in Chapter 3. The coyote is more inclined to use the same trails than are the bobcat or fisher, but all can be caught in their tracks

Figure 5–11 A bit of woodland drama. The signs in the snow indicate where an owl swooped down to catch a mouse, missed, and then skidded along in renewed attempts to catch it.

when those tracks lead to a deer carcass or other bait.

We found where a bobcat had been holing up under a windfall and walking every night to feed on a deer carcass. (We could not determine how the deer had died.) The snow was deep and the cat followed its own track to and from the carcass and had been doing so for quite a while by

Figure 5–12 Dave, minus his beard, hefts a 30-pound bobcat in our backyard.

the look of it. A trap slipped under one of the cat's tracks in the snow so that the trap pan barely broke through the snow at the bottom of the track caught that cat the first night out.

The idea of simply slipping a trap into the snow and under an animal's track so that the trap pan rests just below the track is different from the method described in Chapter 3. It can be done under conditions of dry snow, and it may be the only choice if you are not prepared with wax paper or other winter trap covering. To do it, dig a tunnel in the snow from one side and angle right under the animal's track. The trap is then placed in this tunnel and under the animal's track. The larger the trap size, the better it will function under the snow. Have the trap pan right in the bottom of the track and the trap wired to a drag or solidly to a nearby tree.

When making a trail set for coyote that is coming to bait, whether that bait is a natural one such as a deer carcass or one that you have put out, make your set 100 yards or more from the bait (this is not necessary for bobcat or fisher). This distance is even more important if you are using the more visible snare. The closer a coyote gets to bait, the more suspicious and watchful it gets.

The carcasses of several deer scattered over one's trapline are a real help in trapping coyote, bobcat, and fisher. Even when all that remains are bones, the coyote will return again and again as it makes its rounds. Sometimes a pack of six or seven coyotes will visit such a spot. I like to have traps or snares set in the several trails that invariably lead to the carcass. Snowfalls will cover these trails and I may have to make adjustments such as raising the snares, but I never consider pulling them. Sooner or later the pack will come swooping through. Double, even triple catches can be made at such times. Bear in mind, that "trails" are single sets of tracks in the snow. And even though these tracks will be buried from view by new snowfalls, the coyote, or coyotes, will come trotting down the now invisible trail placing each foot almost exactly as before. This phenomenon never ceases to amaze me.

Snaring

Snaring, where legal, can be a highly effective means of catching the coyote. We treated all of our snares to a bath in boiling logwood dye. This would replace the odor of steel with that of a natural wood odor and impart a dark coloring to match the twigs and branches among which the snare would be set. They can also be whitewashed, which, I'm told, makes them almost invisible and was popular with at least one well known trapper, O.L. Butcher.

I was tempted to whitewash some of our snares, but wasn't sure how to go about it. My main concern was that paint of any kind might emit an odor. Besides, in years past I'd done well using snares that were not treated in any way. I believe that the shine of a new snare is a deterrent, however. Worse is to use new snares that have a protective coating of oil, which new snares normally have. Untreated snares should at least be boiled to remove any oil, or left out in the weather for a few weeks.

Figure 5–13 I set a snare where a coyote has run under a fallen tree.

It is hard for some to believe that the trap-wise coyote will put its head in the exposed noose of a snare, but they will and do. At night or in the early hours of morning and dusk, when they are most active, coyotes will scarcely notice the thin lines of a snare because those lines blend in with millions of other thin lines made up of branches, stems, vines, and twigs.

Yet, the cagey coyote will occasionally see the snare or detect a foreign odor. Last winter I had one trot into a snare and halt at the very last moment. From the sign in the snow it appeared to have sat back on its rump. The snare, partially closed, slipped off its nose. I was disappointed, of course, but couldn't help admiring the coyote's clever action. I knew it was unlikely I would ever catch that animal, at least not that winter. One lesson is all it needs.

Deep snow is not a prerequisite for snaring because coyotes will follow certain trails, visible to their eyes or noses only, even during the spring, summer, and fall. But deep snow does encourage them to stick more closely to those trails.

The snare set

I was following a logging trail one day and found a lone coyote track crossing the trail. There was about ten inches of snow on the ground. I started backtracking the coyote, that is, I followed its tracks backward in the direction it had come from instead of where it was going. I looked for other tracks joining the single track. It could be that up to a half dozen coyotes had crossed that logging trail, all running in the one track, but it appeared I was dealing with a lone animal. I looked to see if the track passed between two trees that were close together or a thick clump of brush or briars. I needed a tight spot where I could hang a snare and it would not be easily noticed.

I backtracked the trail because I knew that if and when the coyote returned, it would return from the same direction. They usually make a circular route. I wanted it to encounter my snare before seeing where I had been walking in the snow beside its track. Not that this necessarily would have any meaning for the coyote, but if I'm only going to set one snare I like to do it this way.

Finally I found where the coyote had run through a clump of aspen saplings. The track passed close to one aspen sapling about four inches in diameter, and I wired the end of the snare to it. I formed a noose in the other end of the snare. The noose hung beside the aspen sapling and directly over the coyote's track. The noose was oval shaped—about ten inches from top to bottom and eight inches from one side to the other. The bottom of the snare was approximately eight inches above the bottom of the coyote's track in the snow. I used to snare foxes in the same way, except I would have the noose a little smaller and closer to the ground.

To hold the noose in position, I broke off two sapling stems half the thickness of a pencil and inserted one through each side of the noose and into the snow. See these two stems in position in Figure 5-14.

Next I lay a dead limb against the sapling the snare was tied to. I rested it over the top of the noose. I wanted to encourage the coyote to duck under this limb and into the noose, and any passing deer to step over it. I pushed another small stem into the snow under the noose with the top of the stem touching the bottom of the noose. This was to encourage the coyote to raise its head if it was running with its nose to the ground. Then I backed away from the set and kicked snow into the tracks where I'd been standing and sent a cloud of snow over the whole set. A little of it

Figure 5–14 Snare set.

Figure 5–15 I caught this hefty coyote in a self-locking steel snare.

Figure 5–16 Dave sets out on cross-country skis to check a line of coyote snares.

Figure 5–17 Pelts of coyotes caught in mid-winter like these two brought top prices.

clung to the dead limb above the snare noose and gave it a natural appearance. I'd worn clean gloves while setting the snare. The whole operation took only a few minutes.

The coyote track was fresh and I knew the animal would not return for a week or so. This one returned nine nights later, and I caught it. It was dead in the snare. They usually are in the sub-zero cold of a northern winter. What happens is they loose body heat in fighting to escape. Then, exhausted from struggling, they fall asleep and succumb to the cold within a night. The animals heavy neck muscles prevent its strangling.

Can you simply hang a snare along any coyote track and expect to catch it in nine or ten days? No way. You can hope to catch it, but there is no guarantee. It's really a guessing game. The toughest part is deciding whether or not to leave snares in a spot where coyotes have gone through when weeks go by and there is no sign of the quarry.

I had four snares set where coyotes had circled a gravel pit. There were at least four or five of them and I was sure they would come back, but I became increasingly frustrated after four weeks passed and there was no sign of them. I was ready to pull those snares by the end of the fifth week. Finally they returned, and two of them stayed behind in my snares.

I like to put at least one snare where a pack of coyotes are trailing—that is, running in single file—but it is wise to have a few sets where they have spread out after trailing or are starting to regroup. If you're lucky, you can take two or three animals from a pack. This is good, because chances are you'll never take another from the same pack. In the case of two coyotes traveling together, if you catch one you'll be hard pressed to catch the other that winter. Oh, occasionally you'll catch one that is trap-wise, but they don't often make mistakes.

The greater share of snares I set on coyote tracks that winter did not produce coyotes or even come close. Yet, when I did connect, it all seemed so easy.

6

Otter
and Beaver

It was a week before the opening of the otter trapping season when I found otter sign where two creeks joined. One bank was plastered with the pasty, gritty droppings left by them. There was an old beaver den here that was part bank den and part lodge. I suspected that otter were entering it from an opening below the ice.

The otter season ran December 1 through December 15 with a limit of three animals per trapper. This seemed like the perfect location to catch at least part of that limit.

There were several narrow openings in the creek ice where otter had been swimming. I could see where one or more had crawled out onto the ice to enter the next opening, and the one after that. The jaws of a 330 Conibear trap would just fit into that largest opening, making for a perfect blind set.

Three days before the otter season opened I returned to check some snares I'd set nearby for coyote. All the openings in the ice had frozen except the one where I planned to set a Conibear trap. Swift flowing water below this opening prevented its freezing. After checking my snares, which were empty, I crossed the creek below the opening in the ice and stepped onto the frozen surface of the second, smaller creek.

Surprise! The ice collapsed under my feet and I was suddenly

A MODERN TRAPLINE

waist-deep in water in a creek that couldn't have been more than four feet across. The ends of my long, sheep-lined coat floated around me as creek water poured into the tops of my hip boots. The air temperature was 27 degrees below zero.

It probably took 30 maddening seconds to extricate myself from that icy little creek. Every layer of clothing was saturated. I lay back in the snow and stuck my feet in the air to drain water from my hip boots. Then I headed in the direction of the road and my truck, about a quarter mile away. I'd have been in serious trouble in a true wilderness situation. As it was, I was simply disgusted. I would have to return home for dry clothes.

As I reached my truck all feeling had left my feet. I wrenched off my boots and socks and replaced them with a dry pair of each I keep in the truck. I wished I had extra wool pants and underwear because I couldn't continue without them. I headed for home with the heater blasting and my teeth chattering. From that day on, I have kept a complete change of clothing in my truck.

The weather continued bitterly cold; in fact, it was the coldest winter in the recorded history of our state. When I returned on the opening day of otter trapping season, the opening in the ice where I planned to set a Conibear trap was frozen. Remembering Charlie's advice about clearing ice from a set and making a catch before it froze again, I chopped another opening.

I cocked a 330 Conibear trap and, with the springs straight out to the sides, set the trap in the water. The springs rested on the frozen surface on each side of the long, narrow opening in the ice. The trap did not set deep enough. I tilted the springs downward, putting the trap at the right depth. It sat surprisingly rigid. The trigger wires just barely grazed the surface of the water.

I believed an otter would point its nose between the wires. If it dived below the surface to avoid them it would trip the trigger with its back. I covered the trap springs with snow. A length of old snare wire was attached to the trap and then tied to a six-foot pole that I laid in the snow by the bank. Using a drag with a water set may seem strange, but I reasoned any otter attempting to escape would do so below the ice and the drag could not be pulled through the small opening in the ice.

When I checked this set, the trap was frozen solidly in the creek ice. I chopped it free, then further opened the ice. I reset the trap. It was bitterly cold work and I had little hope that it would remain open more than two hours.

Two days later it was a repeat performance. I chopped the trap free, cut another long opening in the ice, and reset the trap.

The next time I checked the set the ice was again frozen solid, but this time the trap and drag were gone. For a moment I thought the trap was stolen, but something about the creek looked different, even under several inches of new snow. The frozen surface appeared to have caved in or been shattered in some way, although it was now frozen solid. Then I noticed a pole sticking out of the ice about 20 yards downstream. Could it be my drag?

Ten minutes later I removed from the water, pole, trap, and a 20-pound female otter. The otter had been caught far back on the body instead of across the neck or chest and had put up a terrific struggle. It broke its way through 20 yards of three to four inch ice before succumbing.

Blind sets

The set that caught the otter was one of many variations of blind sets that will take otter. In the case of the 330 Conibear trap, there are also variations of how the trap could have been set—upside down, sideways, on a pole vertically, or on a pole horizontally.

Otter will take overland shortcuts across sharp bends in rivers and streams. A good-sized animal, the trail they leave in traveling overland is easily seen. Their tracks resemble fox or small dog tracks. Other signs are their droppings and vomit, which are full of fish scales. Set one or two No. 3 or 4 leg-hold traps in likely locations. Since an otter's feet commonly are tucked in when swimming, set the traps in four to six inches of water for a hind leg catch.

Beaver ponds attract otter. A narrow break in an old dam is a good location for a trap. If the pond is frozen, look for spring holes, rapids, or other openings where otter are entering and exiting the water.

Channel sets

A good location for an open water set is where a feeder stream comes into a large river or lake. Before the season, find where a log is lying across the stream close to the surface so that the otter has to dive under the log to get past it. Then narrow the sides with guide sticks so that the opening is about one foot wide. Guard this space under the log and between the guide sticks with a 330 Conibear trap when the season opens. Otter are not reluctant to pass through small openings and, in fact, seem to seek them out.

Figure 6–1 This is the otter I caught in a 330 Conibear trap set in a narrow opening in creek ice.

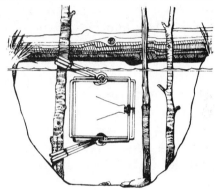

CHANNEL SET

BLIND SET

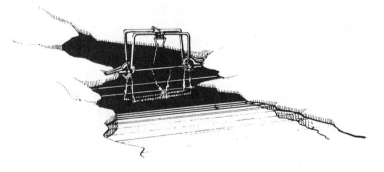

Figure 6–2 Otter sets.

109

Under-ice pole sets

Beaver trapping opened December 1 and continued through February 28. We didn't set a trap, however, until January 7. There weren't enough hours in the day, what with running traps for the other animals. At that, our first set was a disaster.

It started out well enough. Dave and I cut a hole in river ice near a beaver's bank den. We knew about the den, having seen it in the early fall while running traps for fox and raccoon. It was invisible now under a heavy shroud of snow. Even those trees cut in the fall for its winter food supply were barely noticeable.

The water was nine feet deep, much deeper than most beaver ponds. We cut a pole about 12 feet long and put it in the water along with a Conibear trap and freshly cut aspen (popple) for bait. The pole was positioned straight up and down with the trap and bait just below the ice. See Figures 6-4 and 6-5 showing the trap and bait. Wire was used to hold the bait sticks, and the trap jaws also helped to hold them. It looked appetizing, to a beaver that is, and I was confident we would have one when we checked this set.

Dave helped me build this set, but when I checked it I was alone. It was just as well. When I cut away the ice around the bait pole, the only thing to retrieve was the top three feet of the pole. The remaining nine feet of pole along with the trap (and no doubt a beaver) were missing. I realized what happened.

We'd caught a beaver, probably a big one, and in its struggle to escape it broke the pole. Trap, pole, and beaver had sunk to the bottom and drifted downstream. The loss could have been prevented had I tied a length of wire between the trap and that portion of the pole above the ice. Better yet, I could have tied the wire to a pole lying crossways over the hole in the ice.

In most beaver ponds the water is rarely over five feet deep, the bottom being soft mud. In these instances, with the bottom of the pole sunk into the mud and the top frozen in the ice, there is a solid foundation for the Conibear trap. In our ill-fated set, the bottom of the pole rested on a firm sand bottom in nine feet of water with a strong current. The bottom of the pole was probably jerked free when the beaver, a powerful animal, struggled. With nine feet of the twelve-foot pole swinging below the ice, it broke. I never took a chance like that again.

We did little beaver trapping that winter because we'd heard there would be a spring season. The spring season did materialize, running

Figure 6–3 With an ice chisel, I cut a hole in thick river ice, the first step in under-ice beaver trapping.

Figure 6–4 Here I'm adding freshly cut aspen branches, favorite bait for beaver.

Figure 6–5 The set is now ready to be lowered into the water. Trap and bait should set just below the ice.

113

from March 17 through April 30, but we continued having to make under-ice sets until the last ten days or so of the season. It was a tough winter for trapping.

When using the leg-hold trap with a baited pole, it is necessary to have the pole on a slant. The pole should be about four feet longer than the depth of the water and should be dead or dry wood to prevent beaver from gnawing through it. One end is sharpened to drive into the bottom. The bait should consist of a bundle of green aspen twigs, with at least one section of two-inch thick limb. Position this bait so it is just under the water when the pole is pushed into the bottom (see Figure 6-6). I think it is important to wire the bait very firmly in place. All too often a beaver will pull the bait free on the first tug and catch a stick in the trap.

The trap, preferably a No. 4 Oneida or Blake & Lamb under-spring trap (currently the widest-jawed traps available, short of wolf or bear traps), is loosely wired to the pole right under the bait. The trap should pull free once a beaver is caught, but be securely connected to that portion of the pole above the ice with at least three strands of hay wire. I found that old snare wire that was twisted and kinked from catching coyote worked well. The trap pan must be set light because the beaver will be partially floating while feeding on the bait and won't have much weight.

It is very important to place the set in the water about on a 60-degree angle so the beaver will use the area of the pole below the bait as a base to place its feet. This is almost exclusively a front-foot set. Frankly, I had my share of problems with it. I caught beaver, but I'd like to have a dollar for everytime I found the trap set off and empty. A better arrangement is to build a platform for the trap. This can be a nuisance to build but there is less chance of the trap's being set off by the beaver's belly or tail. I'd heard of trappers carrying a triangular piece of two-by-four, wiring it to the bottom of the trap and then lightly nailing it to the side of the slanting bait pole. I found this worked very well.

The problem with trapping beaver with leg-hold traps is positioning the trap at just the right depth (and, in open water, just the right distance from shore) so that the beaver will put a front or rear foot into the trap without first tripping the trap with its body or tail. Even then you can miss it because the hind feet are so large that they can come down on the trap pan and jaws all at the same time and be thrown clear by the closing jaws. The smaller the trap size, the greater is the problem. I used No. 3 Oneida under-spring traps and sorely wished I had No. 4s.

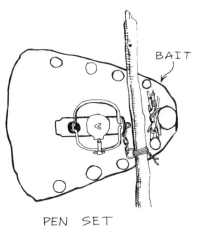

PEN SET

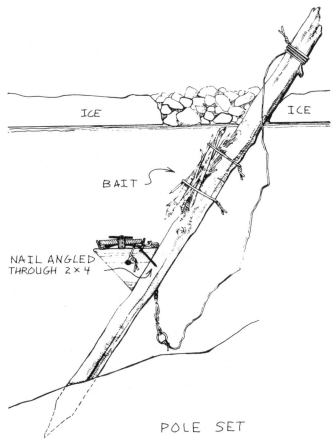

ICE   ICE

BAIT

NAIL ANGLED
THROUGH 2×4

POLE SET

Figure 6–6 Under-ice beaver sets with leg-hold traps.

115

Pen sets

A pen set is an under-ice set made along a bank in the shallower water where beaver are known to travel. It's a good set for creeks. Cut out the ice in a V or U shape over about two feet of water. The open side of the pen should face midstream. Shove dead sticks into the water and mud to make a pen. The tops of the sticks should be above the ice level. The front or open end of the pen should be about 12 inches wide. Securely fasten a fresh piece of aspen or a bundle of twigs and buds to a stouter dead limb and press this down into the mud at the back end of the pen until the bait is touching bottom.

Place one or two leg-hold traps on the bottom so the beaver will step on them in its effort to reach the bait or while it is attempting to tear it loose. The traps can be wired to a pole lying across the opening in the ice, or better yet, a tree or root along the shore. Charlie Mechley claimed he made this set in water up to six feet deep. The trap was lowered into the water by the connecting wire and then flopped right side up on the bottom.

When making under-ice sets for beaver, it is usually advisable to fill in the hole with ice and snow. If the weather has turned mild, it is advisable to attach a crossbar to the pole to prevent the trapped animal from pulling the pole under the ice and thereby escaping with your trap and pole. Normally the pole will freeze in and no crossbar is needed.

Open water sets

There are long periods in the winter when beaver move very little. But then comes that exciting time when the ice melts free of the edge of a beaver dam and little openings appear along the shorelines of lakes. This is the time to trap beaver. They are ravenous for fresh aspen in the East and cottonwood in the West, and their fancy turns to thoughts of love.

"Are they running yet?" the fur buyer asked as I brought in the pelts of three beaver I'd caught and skinned that morning.

"You bet," I replied.

"You know," the buyer continued, "for a while there they weren't moving at all. I hardly got a single beaver one week. Now I've got beaver pelts piled all over the place."

Those last two weeks of the season were fun. I trapped alone at this time, but in the evenings I would tell Dave all about it. I was particularly happy to report the taking of a beaver just outside of town and along a major highway. A few days before, I'd braked the truck to swing into a roadside cafe when I noticed fresh beaver cuttings. Now beaver do not go around felling trees in the spring as they do in the fall. In the spring it is more a discreet nibble here and there, and aquatic vegetation makes up most of their summer diet. But I'd seen fresh cutting, so I parked the truck and walked back along the highway.

There was cattail swamp on both sides of the highway with just a little open water here and there. I noticed some aspen cuttings on a tiny island, probably from the fall before, but there were gnawed sticks in the water that looked fresh. I wondered if there might be a culvert under the highway. There was.

I headed back to the truck and got out a Conibear trap, setting it at one end of the culvert. All this while cars and trucks roared by within a few feet of me. I was a little nervous about having the trap stolen in such a spot, but I went ahead with the set, making it much like the channel set described for otter. I used guide sticks to narrow the culvert and force the beaver to pass through the jaws of the trap.

Two days later I stopped to check this set and the trap was gone. My first thought was that it had been stolen, but the trap had not been staked very solidly, nor had I used a safety wire. It just wasn't the kind of spot where you were likely to lose a beaver caught in the Conibear trap. Then I saw a portion of trap jaw sticking out of the vegetation only ten yards away. I also saw the webbed hind foot of a beaver between the jaws. Somehow the beaver had got caught by a leg in the body-gripping Conibear trap. It didn't get far before becoming entangled, however, and was drowned.

What I enjoyed most during those spring days was hiking to a beaver pond that was about two and one-half miles back in the woods. I had this pond to myself and it contained a lot of beaver, but half the fun was looking for animal tracks on the way to it (there was still snow on the ground). There were timber wolves in the area of the pond, and I found tracks of bobcat and fisher. Then one day I became concerned about the wolves.

I had left the skinned carcass of a beaver near the beaver dam and the wolves found it and ate it. From then on they patrolled the edge of the dam whenever they were in the neighborhood. If they found a beaver in one of my traps I had no doubt they would tear it loose and eat it.

I walked anxiously from one set to another when I saw their tracks, fearing I would find only fragments of fur instead of a beaver. But all my traps were anchored in deep water and drowned beavers were out of sight. One day the wolves patrolled only half the dam, which was

117

fortunate, because on the other side lay a blanket-sized beaver drowned in only a foot of water. The wolves would have seen it easily. I'd anchored the trap in deep water but the beaver became entangled in brush near shore.

Bait sets

I caught the big beaver in a baited set. The water was normally quite deep right up to the edge of the dam, but in this spot there was an underwater ledge about ten inches down that extended for several feet into the pond. I set two traps on the ledge. They guarded a half-dozen sticks of fresh aspen that I wedged into the edge of the dam. I stuck a few guide sticks into the bottom in such a way as to force the beaver over my traps in order to reach the bait. There was still ice on the pond with small openings like this one along the dam, and the beaver were hungry for fresh food. I caught the beaver by a hind foot.

Many trappers build a good bait set for beaver with six green aspen sticks, a minimum of one inch thick, pushed into the bottom next to a bank where the water is over twelve inches deep. Set a leg-hold trap against the bottom of the sticks, with the loose jaw facing out. To catch the hind foot, place a second trap about sixteen inches from the bait. Use solid dead sticks to stake both traps. When using a Conibear trap with a bait set, guide sticks are especially useful in directing the beaver into the trap.

Scent mound sets

As soon as they can get on shore in the spring, beaver begin posting their area with "scent mounds." These are patties of mud mixed with grass or leaves and anointed with sweet-smelling castor. This is a brownish, unctuous substance with a strong, penetrating odor secreted by certain glands in the groin of the beaver. Its purpose is to alert a wandering adult beaver that a suitable mate may be waiting nearby. They are sure-fire set locations.

If the bottom is shallow and gently sloping, I'll set a trap where the depth reaches ten to twelve inches. After setting the trap and anchoring it to a pole or rock in deep water, I'll add a few guide sticks, putting two or three on each side of the trap. I don't have the trap in the center of the guide sticks, but rather a little to one side and in line, I hope, with a beaver's hind foot. Such deep-water sets rarely catch mink or muskrat that are usually closed to trapping in the spring.

118

Figure 6–7 I lured this big male into a trap using the castors and glands from a female beaver. It probably weighed between 50 and 60 pounds.

I caught a big male beaver in an old mine lake in such a set. (See Figure 6-7). The set was an imitation of the scent mound left by a beaver. I'd caught a large female beaver in another lake and when I skinned it, I cut away the sexual organs and castors, easily removed by pulling the whole business away from the lower crotch area of the beaver and cutting away the thin tissue that connects it to the body. I lay this in an old beaver trail I found along the shore of the mine lake and a few inches from the water. First, though, I set a handful of grass and leaves on the ground. I lay the castors and organs on this dry material and cut them open with my knife to release the odor. Then I placed a little mud from the lake bottom on top. Any beaver swimming by would smell it, swim toward the shoreline to investigate it, and put its foot in the trap. The next day I had the big male.

I found that as more and more open water became available and natural foods easily obtained, beaver were less interested in bait. But the scent mound set, either real or artificial, almost always worked.

Blind sets

I also caught beaver in blind sets. For example, I caught one where it traveled over a dam to get from one body of water to another. I caught two beaver on one of the mine lakes where they waddled over an old

Figure 6–8 Here I'm lowering a Conibear trap into an underwater channel that I believe beaver are using. The pole rested on the surface of the water and forced beaver swimming on the surface to dive under it and into the trap.

road that separated two bodies of water. Then a point of land juts into a beaver pond, there is often a trail crossing it that is used as a short-cut by the beaver. Trails used by beaver are easily seen. Traps are set in the water, never in the trail.

Sometimes at a set location I would find there was an underwater ledge four to six inches deep right next to shore. I would occasionally set a trap at this depth, hoping for a front-foot catch. The depth for a hind-foot catch might be ten to twelve inches, or sometimes deeper depending on the size of the beaver. Sometimes these connected and sometimes they didn't. This is probably less of a problem for the more experienced beaver trapper. Personnally, I found the 330 Conibear trap to be much more efficient. This killer trap can be placed where the beaver must swim between the jaws to reach bait, scent, trail, or den entrance.

A favorite set with the Conibear trap was to attach it to a pole and then lay the pole horizontally across a narrow channel leading to a lodge or simply in a channel used as a swimming route by the beaver. On encountering the pole lying across the surface, the beaver would dive under and into the trap. Sometimes I would have the trap set quite deep with the pole under water. In this case I lay another pole or two above it to encourage the beaver to dive and go through the opening between the trap jaws. When using the Conibear trap in this way, I usually have the trigger on the bottom. There is some complaint that the trigger mars the important fur on a beaver's back during those few moments it struggles in the trap.

My most memorable catch was made with the Conibear trap. The beaver was a large, blanket-sized female. This catch can be seen in Figure 6-9. Note the beaver lodge in the background and the edge of the dam running from the left edge of the photo to the lodge and beyond.

I discovered this pond while running snares for coyote in the winter months, noting that there were human tracks in the snow leading to the then frozen pond. A pole set had been made near the lodge. When spring came and the ice on the pond began to break up, I walked along the dam looking for possible set locations. I made one set in an obscure spot. The next day I stopped to check this trap and found that three or four traps had been set along the dam that morning. I suspected it was the trapper who had the pole set through the ice the winter before. While it is perfectly acceptable practice for several trappers to all work the same pond, I believed I was crowding this trapper. I decided to pull the trap I'd set and set it elsewhere along the pond. Since the dam was probably the center of activity, this would give the other trapper first crack at the beaver.

121

Figure 6–9 This is the beaver I caught across from the lodge in what I believe was an auxiliary den.

OTTER AND BEAVER

I had my eye on a little point of land that jutted into the pond directly opposite the lodge. This point is seen in the foreground of the picture in Figure 6-9. The ice was opening along this point and I could probably make some kind of set. I found a narrow, but rather deep channel that seemed to disappear within the bank. I wondered if this might be an auxiliary den for the beaver, a place to go when things got too hot around home. I cut a pole and fitted a Conibear trap on it, laying the pole horizontally in the water with the trap below. I set it deep enough so that the bottom of the trap rested on the floor of the deep channel. This put the pole underwater. I was a little concerned that a beaver might decide to go over the pole, so I laid two more poles on top of it. The ends of the poles were held in place by thick vegetation in the shallow water on each side of the underwater channel. Now if a beaver wanted to swim into the point of land, it would have to go through the jaws of the Conibear trap.

Still, I wasn't all that confident about it. For one thing, I didn't know how many beaver the other trapper had caught. Perhaps the pond was even trapped out. This would not be an environmental disaster since we currently have more beaver in our state than the Department of Natural Resources cares to think about. This is the result of low prices paid for beaver pelts. When they get too numerous they cause all kinds of problems, flooding fields, highways, and even homes.

I was heading out to the highway where my truck was parked, walking a rutted tire-track logging trail, when a four-wheel drive vehicle came bouncing along. Two young fellows were in the cab and turned out to be the ones trapping the pond. I then found out that, no, they weren't the ones trapping it last winter. In fact, they just stumbled across it that morning. They were returning to set even more traps. I mentally kicked myself for being "Mr. Nice Guy" and leaving them all that area of beaver dam to trap. And here I'd made only the one set!.

I didn't feel badly at all the next day. The big beaver's feet were sticking out of the water when I came to check the trap. I believe I caught the best animal in the pond. I set my camera on a high stump and with the aid of its self-timer mechanism, took the photo that appears in Figure 6-9.

Taking pictures is often a bother, but like millions of others I'm glad that I took the time later on. In fact, I've made a little photo album from snapshots taken on our trapline. They bring some hazy memories into sharp focus.

Drowning sets

A final word on beaver. A blanket-sized beaver will tip the 50-pound mark. Their strength and resolve are formidable. It is your responsibility to kill the animal as quickly and humanely as possible. I believe I have failed when an animal escapes, since there is a certain amount of damage done.

Beaver are easily drowned in under-ice sets. Be sure that the wire you use to anchor your traps is strong enough to withstand a certain amount of twisting. Beaver cannot exert their full strength underwater and usually drown within ten minutes. Heavier gauge wire is sold by the pound at hardware stores and is reasonably priced. You'll need a lot of it, particularly for open-water trapping.

It is in open-water trapping that beaver sometimes break wire, pull stakes loose, or pull their feet free of a trap. If a beaver is able to gain firm footing on shore or in shallow water, it can exert tremendous force.

There are a couple of ways to handle the anchoring of traps in open-water trapping. One is to make use of the drowning device that comes attached to the end of the trap chain on most large-size traps. Insert a wire through the hole in this device and twist one end of the wire to a stake in shallow water and the other end to a stake in deep water. The wire must slant downward into deep water. When positioned correctly, the drowning device will slide down the wire but not up. When in doubt, simply move the device by pulling on the trap chain. It slides only one way.

Another method is to anchor a long wire to a stake in deep water with no slack between the trap and stake, and then attach a two- to five-pound rock to the wire or trap chain about a foot from the trap. The beaver will attempt to swim away in deep water and when he does, this weight will drag him down rather quickly.

If you find a live beaver in your trap, cut a long pole with a fork at one end and twist this around the trap chain or wire fairly close to the animal and push it down to the bottom, holding it there for ten minutes or until all the struggling stops. If this is impossible, shoot the animal in the head with a .22, angling the shot so the slug will lodge in the beaver's body and there is no exit hole.

7
Additional Sets

We stuck with a few basic sets for each of the animals we trapped. All are good, time-honored sets and are described in Chapters 3 through 6 on those animals. You can stick with those sets and expect to make good catches, but there are other sets for the animals we trapped that will produce equally as well, or are well worth knowing.

Scent post sets

Just as a dog is interested in places where another dog has urinated, so are the fox and coyote. Even the locations are much the same. Any object standing alone on the trail is a potential target for this act.

I look for such places as abandoned railroad grades, sand and gravel pits, woods roads, trails, old cow paths, and fence lines. Look for a natural object that could already be a target. If the ground is sandy or the vegetation otherwise sparse around it, making it an easy place to conceal traps, look no further. Sprinkle one-half ounce of fox or coyote urine on and around it.

Dig in a trap, each with its own drag, on both sides of the object. Cover and conceal the traps as in making the dirt-hole set.

If no natural object is available, plant a dead limb in the ground. Scent posts for fox should be no more than three to five inches high, a maximum of eight inches for coyote. A tuft of meadow grass about four inches high and just as wide, either natural or planted, works well for fox. The male will raise his leg to hit this target. The female will often straddle the tuft of grass to make her deposit.

Brush out all footprints and leave the set looking as natural as possible. Use no bait or lure. This set is exceptionally effective during the mating season and may also be used in the snow.

Mound sets

The mound set is best known as a dog-proof set for catching foxes, but it also works for catching coyotes. Locate an anthill, natural mound, or stump with a rotted surface and conceal a trap on top. Then dump a large bait 10 to 20 feet away and a little downhill if possible. A stray dog will go straight to the bait, but a fox will circle the bait and scramble to the top of the mound to get a better look. Mound and bait should be in some kind of a clearing.

The dirt-hole set is often used with a nearby mound set. If a fox is suspicious of the dirt-hole set, it will often jump on the mound to get a better look. If an animal is already in the dirt-hole trap, a curious fox may jump onto the mound to watch.

One day on our trapline I carried the rib cage of a deer out onto the frozen surface of a pond and left it there. I'd seen coyote tracks circling the edges of the pond. The next time I came by I found the tracks of a coyote in the snow. It had walked to the top of a beaver lodge, a sort of king-size mound, for a better look at the bones. It missed my trap by inches!

Box cubby sets

I like to think this is a set that I originated. It is designed for mink primarily, but I've found it to be an excellent muskrat producer when used along the shorelines of lakes, ponds, and marshes.

The box cubby is a long, narrow box with an opening at each end. It is made from old, preferably weathered wood and imitates a hollow log or almost any narrow opening that mink love to investigate along streams and lake shores. It can be made and set into position on the trapline well before the season opens.

I like to make them from slab wood, sometimes available free from sawmills. Slabs are the initial result of squaring a tree trunk into lumber and have bark on one side. A box made from it really does look like a hollow log. However, almost any old lumber will do as long as it is not oil stained or covered with old paint that might have an odor. The grey, weathered boards found around old homesteads and abandoned farms are good.

Measurements for the box cubby are never exact and don't need to be, but I do insist that the inside measurements be a minimum of six inches square. That way, I can set a No. 110 Conibear trap slightly within either or both the open ends. I cut a two-inch notch on the right-hand side of the opening to fit the cocked spring of the Conibear trap. Leg-hold traps are equally effective. The length of the cubby should be two feet or longer. I like them longer, but they can get very heavy and hard to carry.

Favorable locations for the box cubby are along rivers, streams, and water-filled ditches; wedging the box under an overhanging bank is ideal. There should be one to two inches of water running through the box and high grass from the overhanging bank hanging down over the exposed side of the box. Another good site is amid the tangled debris of a log jam. Mink always investigate such tangles, but it is difficult sometimes to decide where to set a trap. The box cubby solves the dilemma. Pile dead limbs over the box, and make it appear to be a natural opening leading under the tangle of logs and debris.

The box cubby also works on dry land. Wedge it under an overhanging bank along a river sandbar, preferably an inside bend of the river, which is where you normally find a sandbar. Sift an inch or so of sand over the bottom to give the set a natural appearance and provide trap covering.

When I first used this set along lakeshores and marshes, I tried to make it appear to be an abandoned muskrat house. I did this by piling grass and mud on top of the box. I was surprised by the reaction of the local muskrat population. They flocked to the cubby and started adding more vegetation. The first thing they wanted to do was fill in the open ends. My mink set was suddenly a combination set for mink and muskrat.

The box cubby is especially helpful along those shorelines where one can find little in the way of natural blind sets. The fact that it is portable is a real plus. I use no bait or lure with it since it is a blind set, but a touch of mink urine never hurts. If possible, put your box cubbies out a few weeks before season.

Artificial hole sets

Another good mink set that can be used along those shorelines that offer few set locations, and one that can be prepared before season, is the artificial hole set.

Nothing arouses a mink's curiosity more than a hole along the bank of a lake or stream. You can dig such a hole before season and it will improve with age. It can be dug with an inch or two of water in the entrance for a wet set, or dry in a soft dirt or sand bank for a dry set. The trap is set in the entrance. Measurements are roughly six inches in diameter and up to one foot deep. Generally the hole slants upward and bait and lure are placed in back. Mink urine can be used near the entrance. A fresh chunk of fish or muskrat makes good bait.

Snow sets

Fox and coyote expect to dig up from under the snow much of the food they eat, so sometimes I dig a hole a foot or more deep in snow and place a good-sized piece of bait and a triple dose of lure, and on top of the bait set a trap. The hole is then filled in and when the animal digs for the bait, it will usually dig into the trap.

Snow is porous and makes poor trap cover for elusive animals. Traps should be very clean and free of undesirable odors for use in snow, and your footprints should be brushed out for several yards around the set with a fine evergreen bough.

8

Tips from Our Trapline

Guide sticks

The triangular area of sifted dirt in front of the hole in the dirt-hole set will guide a fox or coyote into the concealed trap. But once a catch has been made, the whole area will be torn up and no real guide lines remain to insure that the next animal will place its foot squarely in the trap. To remedy this, lay two stems of timothy or other weed on each side of the concealed trap. These should slant inward toward the backstop with the ends on each side of the bait hole in an inverted V shape. Hold them in place with a little dirt. The fox or coyote will step between the two stems and into the trap.

Such guide sticks can be used at dirt-hole sets made in sandy spots where no sod has been removed. Earlier in the book, I mentioned a Michigan trapper who made his dirt-hole sets in the sand dunes along Lake Michigan. As I recall, he used tiny pebbles on each side of the trap to guide the animal's foot.

All this may seem incongruous to the newcomer to trapping. The idea that anything would be influenced by a twig or blade of grass is hard to swallow. It is true, however. A comparison is found in the skilled deer hunter who places his feet with care lest he snap a dry twig. Wild animals

129

live every minute of their lives in the fields, woodlands, and waterways, and are influenced by even the minute aspects of their environment. The predators who must depend on stealth and cunning for their survival are influenced even more.

Stakes

For a while I used long aspen saplings for staking mink and muskrat traps. Because they stuck far out of the water it was easy to find my sets. Unfortunately, it was easy for trap thieves to find them as well. I started using shorter stakes and pushing them out of sight below the surface of the water. Whenever it was possible, I wired the end of the trap chain to a tree root, usually below water level.

The possibility of trap thieves influenced me in deciding whether to stake a trap for raccoon, fox, bobcat, or coyote, or use a drag. If the set was in the open where a passing motorist, hunter, hiker, or, in the winter months, snowmobiler might see a trapped animal, I often used a drag. That way the animal would leave the open area and tangle up in the nearest woods, increasing the chances of its not being seen. This was a particularly good ploy in trapping raccoon in roadside culverts.

Skinning

When caught in the fall months, raccoons, foxes, and coyotes are almost always alive in the trap. These animals are a lot easier to skin if you do the job while the carcass is still warm. Never attempt to skin an animal that is even partially frozen. If you plan to use a carcass for bait (muskrat and beaver both make good bait for a variety of other animals), you can keep the carcass around for a longer period of time without its rotting if you remove the entrails and hang it in a cool, shaded spot.

Snares

One of the pluses for using snares is that they are so lightweight. I could carry a dozen or more in a large pocket in my parka and hardly notice the weight. This was much handier than carrying them in my pack sack, but it is also a good way to get foreign odor on snares. I got away with it for quite awhile because I was snaring in continuous sub-zero temperatures that nullified all but the strongest smells. Then the weather warmed and coyotes started detecting my snares. I won't make the same mistake next year. Oh, I'll still carry them in my parka pocket, but each snare will be in an individual sealable plastic bag.

Gloves

I'd have given a lot for a pair of shoulder-length rubber gloves on our trapline. It wasn't so bad making water sets for mink, muskrat, and raccoon during the early fall months. It was murder, though, making sets in small openings in the ice during December. Handling the wet vegetation inside muskrat feeders was even worse. Wrist-length rubber gloves simply don't do the job.

Baiting

Large baits are quickly found by coyotes and foxes when placed out in the center of frozen back country lakes and rivers. Predators often follow lake shores and rivers. You can help them discover the bait even sooner by propping a raven wing in the snow near the bait. The black wing will show up for a long distance against the white snow. Another ploy is to stick a long pole in the snow by the bait. It's in the canine's nature to walk out and check such a pole for the smell of urine, much like a dog will check every fire hydrant.

Several traps attached to drags are used at such a set. They should be set back from the bait to avoid catching crows, ravens, or birds of prey attracted to the bait.

Killing

A stout stick with a fork on one end is good for dealing with small, live caught animals like mink and muskrat. Rap the animal sharply over the head with the straight, preferably smooth end of the stick and then hold it under water with the forked end until all movement ceases.

A word about killing a trapped fox. I prefer to shoot them with a .22 the same as I would a raccoon or coyote. Another way is to stun the trapped fox by rapping it across the nose with the handle of the shovel used in making sets. Then pin the animal's neck to the ground with the grip end of the shovel and kneel or step on the side of the fox's chest. With the lungs collapsed, death comes within seconds. This prevents blood at the set, the fur is not damaged, and it is as humane as any method.

9

Planning
for Next Year

There isn't a doubt in my mind Dave and I would double our catch if we were to run another fulltime trapline. We know, for example, that we have to concentrate our efforts for raccoon along the major rivers in our area. Little preseason scouting is required. Sets would simply be made every quarter mile or so. Raccoon are easy to trap. The secret is the use of good, strong-smelling bait placed where they will detect it. Nothing will stop the raccoon once it gets wind of food. If the trapper has done his part and made a set that guides the animal into a trap that is lightly concealed and securely staked or wired to a hardwood drag, that raccoon is on its way to the drying board.

Because we continued trapping into the winter months, we know the whereabouts of more mink than ever. We often found their tracks in the snow. Nevertheless, we would put in more preseason scouting for them than we had the opportunity to do on our last trapline. Because the mink season opens in late fall, within a week or two of freeze-up, we would have many set locations chosen or prepared before season. No matter how good you are at trapping mink in conditions of ice, snow, and sub-zero cold, you're going to catch more early in the season.

In Chapter 7, I describe two sets for mink, the box cubby and the artificial hole. Both of those sets can be prepared before season. We

Figure 9–1 Dave inspects one of our cubbies, built before season in a remote area, for signs of visiting furbearers.

didn't have the opportunity to employ either on our trapline. We were too involved in preparing for raccoon, an animal that was still a mystery to us. We would spend far less time preparing for the relatively easy-to-catch raccoon and use that time in preparing for mink, making good use of the artificial hole and box cubby sets.

I don't think we could improve much on the preseason preparations we did for fox and coyote, except to have more deep-woods set locations. Because of the high prices paid for the pelts of these animals, the easy-to-reach locations are trapped out or are experiencing heavy trapping pressure. I would rather have a few good sets in deep-woods locations than the hassle of many traps near a roadside.

Another reason for more deep-woods trapping is that coyotes in particular leave the open farm fields once winter sets in and range more in deep woods. I would want to have plenty of dirt holes dug in deep-woods locations so I could continue using them into the winter months. It's hard to dig new sets in ground that is frozen rock hard. I would have a good supply of antifreeze and dry dirt. The antifreeze would, of course, be of the odorless kind used for trapping.

I know we would take the time to experience more open-water trapping for muskrats. We would use our boat and motor on the larger lakes and canoe the small lakes and ponds. We would use the Conibear trap almost exclusively and make good use of bait and lure. This would

Figure 9–2 Dave takes note of a beaver lodge built along a riverbank. We would return to trap this and other spots for beaver.

provide more than variety to our trapline—there has been good money in muskrat trapping in recent years.

But, like most trappers today, I doubt I'll be able to devote the time to a fulltime trapline. More likely I'll have to squeeze in part-time trapping. My work as an outdoor writer requires my spending a lot of time in hunting, fishing, and related outdoor pursuits. But once deer season is over and most of those outdoor pursuits grind to a halt, I have plans.

I'm going to operate a fairly extensive winter trapline. Principal targets will be fox, coyote, bobcat, and fisher, a fascinating group if there ever was one. This will be almost exclusively deep-woods trapping. I'm fortunate to live in a state where you can walk for many miles in some areas without encountering a road. The only persons who penetrate this kind of terrain are snowmobilers, and they stick closely to established trails. I'll make my own trails on snowshoes. I'll make long, circular lines that take all day to walk. I might even make a crude shelter or two so that I can extend the length of some of my lines.

There are advantages to my plan. For one thing it's going to keep me in good physical condition. I really enjoyed the shape I got into on our trapline. Life is a lot more fun when you've got the energy to enjoy it. I'm going to find more of the animals I'm after on a deep-woods trapline. This is especially true of bobcat and fisher. And I expect to have little trouble with trap thieves of any kind. Very few people are willing to venture more than a quarter mile from the nearest road or established trail, especially in the winter. And in many instances I'll get first crack at wide-ranging animals before they get near the roadside and the roadside trappers.

In fact, I'm already planning routes through some wild stretches of country. If you look for them, you can find some pretty wild stretches of country in almost every state and province. With the increase in trapping pressure, it's going to be those trappers who are willing to work that reap the rewards. And those rewards go far beyond money. Almost any job you can think of pays more money than trapping, but few offer the thrill of close encounters with wild animals in wild terrain.

10
Trapping Other Animals

Skunk

The year was 1947, and I was 13 years old. If I played my cards right and managed to dispatch the big striped skunk in my trap, I just might live until my fourteenth birthday, only a couple of weeks away. But I doubted if I would get through the ordeal unscathed. It wasn't so bad when the skunk kept its eyes on me. It was when it threatened me with that upraised tail that things got sticky.

I was trying a new method: you tie a noose to a long pole, slip the noose over the skunk's head, then lift it off the ground. This, I had read, renders a skunk defenseless, as it must brace its feet on solid ground in order to emit its vile smelling spray (untrue). I had been catching more than my share of this defensive essence that fall, a deep lung full of which can knock a man out temporarily and leave him with a severe headache. This defensive liquid, which can be sprayed eight to ten feet, owes its overpowering nature to a sulphide it contains. Getting the liquid in the eyes can be very serious, and it has been known to cause permanent blindness in both humans and dogs.

But if I was aware of these facts at the time, I did not let them bother me. Any kid, halfway agile on his feet, could out-dodge a skunk's aim.

Figure 10–1 Skunk.

Unfortunately, the odor hangs in the air and usually attaches itself to one's clothing no matter what.

So far this particular skunk was putting up with my antics but getting more and more irritated. I could get the noose over its head, but when I attempted to tighten the slip knot, the noose would slip off the animal's head. It was a fool thing to try to do at night anyway. The only light was that cast by an autumn moon. But I gave it one more try and this time pushed the skunk a little too far.

I felt a dimpling of moist drops trace across my forehead like machine gun fire. I stumbled back out of range. The air was filled with essence of angry skunk.

This is not to be confused with the distant, diluted odor one occasionally notices in the evening in the countryside. This close range smell is like walking into a brick wall. It takes your breath away. It turns the stomachs

137

of the faint hearted and will stop the hungriest beast of prey. It will even give pause to a 13-year-old trapper.

Abandoning the noose, I reverted to my usual method of dispatching skunks: I tossed a stick beyond the critter to distract its attention, then raced in and struck the slow-witted animal above the nose with a stout club. This is usually enough to kill a skunk quickly. However, as in this case, the skunk's last convulsive movements are often enough to cause more ejection of liquid which may get on the fur, making the skinning job an extra tough one.

A well placed .22 slug would have eliminated the need for all these wild goings-on, but my home base was the city of Minneapolis. And, although there were woodlands and fields beyond the fringes of town, I wasn't allowed to tote a rifle on my trapline. Still, for the most part, I managed to stay remarkably free of odor, at least I thought so. With all its drawbacks, I found skunk trapping to be a fascinating outdoor experience. It is unfortunate, I think, that there is so little demand for this durable fur today.

Skunks range in size from the one- to two-pound spotted skunk to the hefty ten-pound striped, hooded, and hog-nosed skunk. All are capable of emitting a vile stream of musk from twin jet nozzles located just inside the anal tract.

Many thousands are taken each year in dirt-hole sets made for foxes and coyotes. My favorite set was the cubby set, a three-sided, roofed enclosure with one end left open for the animal to enter and the trap to be set. These were made from logs, rocks, old boards, or whatever was available.

Some of my favorite set locations were near old abandoned buildings, grown over with high grass and weeds, along railroad tracks, ditches, fencelines, and other areas that had high grass and weeds. These are areas where skunks seek out mice, small birds, eggs, insects of all kinds, and the many other tid-bits that skunks find to their liking.

My sets were baited with chicken heads and entrails obtained from a friendly neighborhood butcher. Tainted baits of all kinds are good, including rotted fish, eggs, and so on.

Many skunks are taken by nailing a piece of bait against a fencepost about ten inches above the ground. Place the trap in front of the bait in such a way that the skunk must pass over the trap to reach the bait. The trap need not be covered.

The No. 1½ jump or long spring trap will hold the largest of skunks. It can be staked solid or attached to a drag. It's probably best to stake solid in most cases to prevent the skunk's crawling into a hole or under a woodpile, either of which could make dispatching the skunk difficult.

Skinning a skunk is not difficult, except that extreme caution is necessary in the area of the animal's crotch. Cutting into a scent gland can be a very distasteful experience. It is especially disheartening if you have managed to kill the skunk without its having cut loose with its defensive spray. Contrary to popular opinion, skunks are extremely clean animals and do not ordinarily have any offensive odor.

Opossum

One of the most useful books on trapping I've read is *Pennsylvania Trapping and Predator Control Methods* by the late Paul L. Failor (Harrisburg, Pa.: Pennsylvania Game Commission, 1974). He has this to say about the opossum:

> "Of all the furbearing animals in the state, the opossum is probably the least respected of the entire group. This unwanted predator-furbearer invaded Pennsylvania more than 60 years ago and now has established himself in such numbers in all counties that he is not only detrimental to all forms of small wildlife but a real nuisance on the trap line as well. His propensity for getting into a good fox or mink set, destroying its usefulness from that time on, creates one of the most common disappointments of a trapper's day. It is generally agreed among trappers that to catch an opossum in a trap set for fox nullifies its intended purpose. The set is usually remade at a nearby location with a clean trap after taking an opossum."

The opossum's overall length is two to three feet, weight is 4 to 12 pounds. The fur color is a grizzled grey or off-white. The tail is bare and prehensile, and the female's belly has a pouch. Low pelt prices is the biggest factor affecting opossum trapping, but not the only one. Opossum pelts are greasy and require as much work as a raccoon pelt that brings ten times as much money. For some, the odor of skunk is preferable to that of opossum. Fox, it would seem, feel the same way, since an opossum in a fox set means a ruined set while the odor of skunk can enhance it.

The opossum prefers fence rows, orchards, abandoned buildings, brush, and junk piles. If the fox trapper knows in advance where he is going to trap, he can take many of the opossum in the area before he sets for fox. This will eliminate ruined sets, thereby increasing the number of working sets available to catch the much more valuable fox.

The suspended-bait set can be made quickly and with little effort. First, locate a trail or den showing fresh sign, tracks, trails, or droppings, then look for a tree or fence post that is very near. Nail or tie a smelly bait onto the tree or post about 12 inches from the ground. (Chicken heads or

139

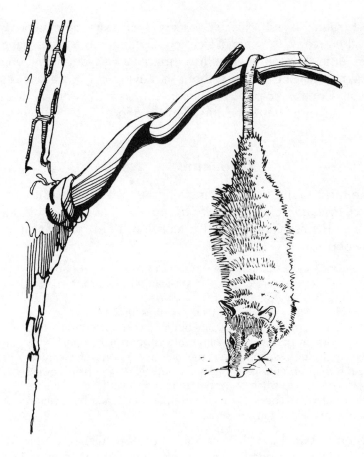

Figure 10–2 Opossum.

entrails make good bait.) Set a No. 1 or 1½ trap below. The trap need not be covered and can be staked solid.

Marten

The marten is a member of the weasel family and has the long, slender lines of the tribe; somewhat larger than the mink, it may weigh up to six pounds.

I recently read of a trapper in southeastern Alaska who trapped 45 marten from a two-mile-long stretch of trapline along the base of a mountain. This struck him as a lot of marten in a very small area. At first he thought this phenomenon unique to southeastern Alaska, with its

Figure 10–3 Marten.

rain-forest environment. However, reliable reports of a catch of over 100 marten from a five-mile-long trapline in the middle Yukon River country, and a take of nearly 200 by an old timer of the upper Yukon dispells such a notion. The trapper's guess was that these apparent high densities reflect a high degree of mobility in marten, especially in males. This will to travel combined with a short food supply at the higher elevations during the winter months is perhaps the explanation.

Marten like heavily forested terrain and high country, usually 4,000 to 7,000 feet altitude in the winter. They are hyperactive, a characteristic of the weasel clan, and seem constantly on the move, probing under windfalls and then, in a flash, flitting through the treetops.

According to several studies, voles and mice are the marten's primary food items, not red squirrels as is so often assumed, but martens are opportunists and it may depend on what is most plentiful at the time. During times of abundance, snowshoe hares become an important food item.

While it has a keen nose and sharp eyes, the marten is not the least bit trap shy. Place a trap in front of bait and the uninhibited marten will fight for the chance to jump into it. A standard set for marten is a natural cubby. A hollow in a tree base serves this purpose very well. Put bait in back and guard the entrance with a trap.

Once the snow starts building up, one must switch to pole sets. This is an easy set to make for martens; it can also be comparatively weather-proof. Select a pine tree with thick protective boughs, and lean a pole against the pine so that the top of the pole is about five feet above the snow. Use your axe to level the top of the pole so that a No. 1½ jump trap can be set. Staple or nail the trap chain to the side of the pine tree. Now nail bait to the pine tree above the trap: red squirrel, rabbit, a skinned-out muskrat, sardines, canned cat food or salmon—almost anything that smells. Bait and trap should be set below thick pine boughs. You can add to the protection against snow by cutting pine boughs and laying them crossways on overhead branches above the bait and trap.

Visibility is important for a good marten set. Select a trap site that can be seen from several approaches. As an added touch, trappers will hang a scented bird wing to flash in the breeze. Scent can be rancid fish or seal oil, with perhaps a little beaver castor thrown in. The essense of skunk is also good. In sub-zero temperatures, bait and lure must be pretty revolting to be noticed.

Trappers in Alaska are finding the No. 110 Conibear trap to be an excellent trap choice for marten as it kills quickly and cleanly. Marten have a thin hide and long, delicate fur, more susceptible to damage than most other furs. The box cubby set (described in Chapter 4) used in conjunction with the Conibear trap and bait should be an excellent set for marten. Use at ground level or prop in the branches of a pine tree.

Wolverine

The wolverine averages about three feet in length and may stand as much as 14 inches at the shoulder. Weight varies between 20 and 35 pounds, but wolverine up to 50 pounds have been reported. The head is broad and the jaws powerful. Color is dark brown to black; two yellow stripes start on each shoulder and meet on the rump.

The wolverine hunts at all hours of the day or night and will take just about anything it can overpower. They are particularly fond of carrion. This liking for carrion makes a slightly "high-smelling" bait a good one.

A good set for wolverine is one where it appears another animal has stashed some food for future use. Find a crevice or hollow and lightly bury bait in the rear of this natural cubby. In some instances you may have to improve on the natural cubby with a few logs or rocks. Traps must be carefully concealed and covered with dirt, snow, or whatever is

Figure 10–4 Wolverine.

the natural material at the set location. Take the same precautions you would in trapping fox or coyote. You can stake the traps solid, but it is usually best to wire them to a heavy drag. Use No. 3 or 4 leg-hold traps.

Weasel

The weasel is the smallest of the furbearing animals sought by the trapper. The least weasel, the smallest of the three kinds of weasel, is seven to eight inches long, including its tail, and weighs only one to two ounces. Even the long-tail weasel, 13 to 18 inches long including its 4- to 6-inch tail, weighs a mere six to nine ounces. The fur is flawless white in winter except for the black-tipped tail.

The weasel, commonly known as ermine in some circles, has long fascinated me. A more fearless, blood-thirsty little demon would be hard to find. Death to mice, rats, gophers, small animals, and birds, the weasel

143

Figure 10–5 This weasel is in its prime winter coat and is about to dine on the much larger snowshoe hare.

is so horrifying to its prey that a fast stepping cottontail rabbit can lose control of its limbs and with piercing screams of terror await the weasel's death-dealing bite to the base of the skull. No clever subterfuge is needed when trapping him—he will boldly step into a bare trap if you lure him with fresh bait.

Outwitting the elements was the real problem in trapping weasels during my days as a schoolboy trapper. Keeping my traps in working order despite freezing and thawing weather and heavy snowfalls kept me busy. I remember the greater weasel I caught in the Red Swamp. Heavy snow had buried all my sets, and I was depressed. Then I scooped away the snow at one set and found a king-sized weasel. I had often heard and read of the various subspecies of weasels, all very similar except for their size, but this was the first really large one I'd seen. I remember I got $2.50 for it, which wasn't bad for 1947. That same year my brother Rich caught the smallest weasel I've ever seen and got $1.60 for it. Nowadays there isn't even a market for weasel.

Years later a friend and I were each to catch weasels that were far larger than the one I caught in the Red Swamp. Mine was a female, the one my friend caught a male and obviously the female's mate. Both were big, but the male was almost as large as a small female mink. Two really beautiful specimens. I would imagine that just the sight of them would freeze a rabbit's heart.

Look for tracks in the snow in grassy ditches, fencelines, cattail swamps, or almost anyplace that high weeds and grass with the accompanying field mice and other small animal life are found.

If ermine ever comes back into fashion, and I suspect that someday it will, I won't waste a moment in building a bunch of box cubbies in which to trap them. For serious weasel trapping, this set is hard to beat. The box cubby is made roughly 6 inches wide, 6 inches high, and 12 inches long, with a 2-inch hole drilled into the front. It looks like a bird house and can be made from scrap lumber or slab wood. The cover is held in place by a single nail at one end so it can be swung to the side to place the bait and trap and to retrieve trapped weasel. The trap is placed below the two-inch entrance hole and the bait in back of the cubby. A No. 1½ trap will catch the weasel around the shoulders and kill it instantly.

Because they are cumbersome, box cubbies are usually set close to the roadside. They will remain in working condition even after heavy snowfalls. A variation is the tin can set. A can that is large enough in diameter to hold a trap in the open end is placed on its side with bait in back and the trap set inside the open end. No trap covering is used at either set.

145

Badger

Broad-shouldered, bowlegged, pidgeon-toed, the badger is built close to the ground and endowed with long digging claws that enable it to dig out and devour all manner of small animals. The loose-fitting hide has long, grizzled, and multicolored hair: grey to white, black and silver-tipped. Head markings are distinctive—a white stripe runs from the nose over the top of the head, the cheeks are white, and in front of each ear is a black slash. The feet are black. Length is two to three feet. Weight is from 12 to 25 pounds.

Badgers prefer the open prairie, but occasionally are found in wooded areas. They are usually most abundant in an area which has a high population of the ground squirrels and small rodents which form the major portion of their diet. In our state, the thirteen-lined ground squirrel (gopher) is the principal kind of ground squirrel, but they are scarce in our area and badgers are only rarely caught.

When they are caught, it is usually in a dirt-hole set made for fox or coyote. The badger has not been of great value for many years, and trappers, particularly Western trappers, have often cursed them for ruining an otherwise good coyote set. Now all that is changing. In a raw fur market report for February 1979, fine-haired badger were listed as selling for $60 to $80, coarse-haired for $20 to $30.

Leg-hold traps No. 3 and 4 are usually recommended for badger. Bait can be meat that is slightly tainted but not spoiled, freshly killed ground squirrels, rabbits, and so on.

Badgers are most often trapped at their dens. Because they do a lot of digging, it is sometimes hard to locate their real den. A home den has a more permanent appearance than the holes dug by the badger in digging out ground squirrels. Look for a well-rubbed hole, often wider than it is high, with pieces of hair around the edges and a worn-down area around the hole.

Set your traps to either side of the hole, as the badger often slides down into the hole and will merely spring a trap set in the center. Conceal your traps with a layer of sifted earth and avoid leaving odors at the set.

When a badger has been digging a lot of holes in an area and you cannot locate its home den, a bait set will often catch it. Put a piece of tainted meat or recently killed ground squirrel in one of the freshly dug holes and conceal a trap in the dirt in front of the hole.

Stake your traps so that the trapped badger cannot get in the hole, or you will have a hard time dragging him back out. A trapped badger is

Figure 10–6 Badger.

quite a fighter, and the trap must be held securely. A badger in a trap can most easily be killed by shooting it in the head with a .22.

Lynx

The lynx can be distinguished from the bobcat by the tail markings. The lynx's tail is tipped with black hairs above and below while the bobcat has black hairs only on top of its tail. The lynx has larger ear tufts than the bobcat and also has larger feet, apparently developed for its life in the deep snow country of the north.

The lynx is found throughout Alaska and Canada and his range blends with that of the bobcat in the northern United States. The lynx, like the wolf, is only able to survive in uninhabited terrain; it prefers heavy forests and is highly dependent on the snowshoe rabbit population, its primary source of food.

Perhaps the most intriguing aspect about the Canada lynx is that whole populations of these northwoods cats can vanish as mysteriously as they appear. Periodic fluctuations of lynx numbers are called cycles. These cycles normally peak when ruffed grouse and snowshoe hares experience peaks in their cycles. The next cyclic high for lynx, hares, and grouse in my home state of Minnesota should occur between 1980 and 1984.

Both bobcat and lynx have similar habits, and the set that takes one will take the other. See Chapter 5.

Figure 10–7 Lynx (left) and bobcat.

11
Combining Hunting and Trapping

When I found mink tracks along the little creek near my deer stand a couple of years ago, I thought of how the money paid for a mink pelt would help defray the cost of the hunting trip. The next morning I was back on stand, but after two hours of trail-watching for whitetails, I headed for the creek with four No. 1½ under-spring traps.

The creek was frozen except for open water below an abandoned beaver dam. It was there that the mink had been most active. Tracks in the snow entered and exited the water in many spots. Some of those spots were too deep to set a trap, but two sites were just right, with two inches of water to cover the trap. I extended the length of each trap chain with wire so I could anchor the trap in deep water. If a mink was caught, the weight of the trap would quickly drown it.

The other two traps I set under and between tree roots that extended out from the bank. Mink always investigate narrow passageways, nooks, and crevices in search of frogs and crayfish. It was the last day of the deer season when I connected—two of the traps held drowned mink.

For many, few things are more conducive to enjoying the outdoors as hunting and trapping. When you combine the two, as I often do, the results can be exhilarating.

A MODERN TRAPLINE

Despite the casualness of this approach to trapping, some preparations are necessary to make it work. Well in advance of the hunting and trapping seasons, I build a box in which to store all my trapping gear. I make it a permanent fixture in my car or truck.

The trapping you squeeze in on hunting trips will not require many traps. However, you never know the kind of furbearer you're going to encounter, so I store traps of several sizes in the box, along with a layer of pine boughs or leaves to help retain an earthy odor. A good way to keep foreign odors from permeating your gear is to keep the box outside your vehicle on a car-top carrier. In the same box I put my trapping tools: small shovel, dirt sifter, hatchet, rubber gloves, and so on. I have a separate compartment for bait and lure bottles and protect them with insulating material.

I remember a few years back when I walked into a clearing in the woods while hunting ruffed grouse. A hole had at one time been bulldozed in the clearing and the resulting earth pile, mostly fine sand, was riddled with fox tracks. Foxes and trappers have an affinity for sand; foxes like to play in it and trappers, because it is easy to dig in and makes good trap covering, like to set traps in it.

I headed out to my truck. At the truck I opened my box of trapping gear and removed a knapsack that already contained a No. 2 coil-spring trap, stake, fox urine, lure, digging tool, hatchet, and bait. The bait was entrails of ducks shot the week before. These, along with some of the feathers, were in individual plastic bags with sealable tops. The contents of each bag was slightly tainted by now and would be very tempting to a fox.

Back at the earth pile I made a dirt-hole set near the base of the pile where the sand leveled out. I made it very quickly since there was no sod to remove and the sand was easy to dig in. The set seemed inconspicuous in the sand, so I made the hole larger than normal and scattered many duck feathers around the completed set. I used fox urine liberally and, as I backed away from the set, sprayed even more urine where I'd been crouched while making the set. I made another set 50 yards away. The next morning the set held a red fox.

The dirt-hole set is useful for the hunter-trapper because it will take a variety of furbearers including fox, coyote, badger, bobcat, and raccoon. Trail and blind sets are also standbys. During winter hunting forays I often switch to the self-locking steel snare.

It's surprising how the whole spectrum of outdoor activities often complement one another. I remember as a youngster I discovered brook trout spawning in a little creek I was trapping for mink. I knew that trout were stocked in the upper waters of the creek, but it was only when I sighted the fall spawning activities of the brook trout downstream, while trapping mink, that I realized this section of creek offered any possibilities. The next summer I caught several nice stringers of trout.

Rarely does a trapping season go by without my discovering potential hunting sites, and while hunting I'm constantly noticing the tracks, trails, and droppings of furbearers. Combining hunting and trapping makes every trip afield doubly interesting.

12
Traps
and Equipment

I like to stick with name brands when buying traps, and two that have stood the test of time are Blake & Lamb and Woodstream. Woodstream sells Conibear, Oneida, Victor, and Newhouse® traps as well as Havahart® and Tender Trap® cage traps used by some trappers in special situations.

Conibear traps

Conibear traps are designed to grip the animal about the neck or chest, killing it with the blow. On our trapline this occurred a high percentage of the time.

These body-gripping traps are widely used by trappers throughout the United States and Canada. Their experience proves that a variety of successful sets can be made in holes, runways, cubbies, and on rafters and poles. In addition, these traps work equally well on the ground, suspended, submerged in water, under ice, or when covered with light snow. A wire trigger permits Conibear traps to be baited or used for blind sets. However, they should never be used where they may take nontarget animals, such as dogs or protected game.

They come in four sizes: No. 110, 120, 220, and 330. The only difference between the No. 110 and No. 120 is that the 120 is equipped with double springs. "Series 2" Conibear traps are now available with rounded corner loops and other improvements, including a quick safety release feature on the 220 and 330-size traps. (In case you trap a non-target animal such as yourself, you can release the trap with one hand.) Proper and safe setting of the 220 and 330 Conibear traps is shown in Figure 12-3. The smaller Conibear traps can be set with your hands.

We found the 110 size with its single spring to be more than adequate

Figure 12-1 No. 110-2 and 120-2 Conibear Series 2 traps. (Courtesy of Woodstream Corp.)

 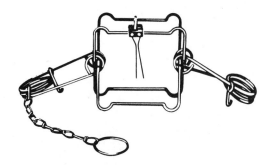

No. 110-2 Conibear   No. 120-2 Conibear

Figure 12-2 No. 220-2 and 330-2 Conibear Series 2 traps. (Courtesy of Woodstream Corp.)

 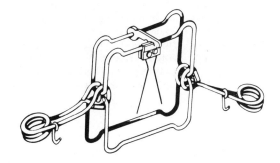

No. 220-2 Conibear   No. 330-2 Conibear

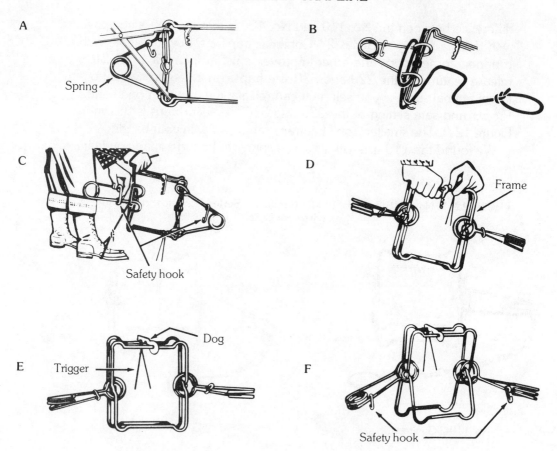

Figure 12–3 Setting the Conibear 220 and 330 traps. (Courtesy of Woodstream Corp.) A. Extend both springs so they are pointing directly away from trap. Hook notched ends of setting tool over spring loops and compress. Set spring safety hook to keep spring compressed. Repeat for second spring. B. If a trap setting tool is not available, an 8-foot section of ¼-inch rope can be used as shown. Tie loop in one end of rope and thread other end through spring eyes. C. Place foot through loop and pull other end of rope to compress springs. D. Pull frames together with one hand. E. Position trigger and dog at desired location along frame and then set trigger in preferred notch of dog. F. Be sure trigger is secure within notch of dog. Place trap in desired location. Then, keeping hands clear of trap frames, slowly release each safety hook and slide to coiled ends of spring. Trap is now ready for use.

for mink and muskrat. Also, it is easier to conceal. According to the manufacturers, the No. 110 is suitable for muskrat, mink, weasel, squirrel, and spotted skunk, the No. 120 for mink and animals of similar size.

154

The No. 220 Conibear trap is more powerful than needed for mink and muskrat, and probably a bit light for heavy raccoon, beaver, and otter. It is my guess that it would be ideal for fisher. It would be useful as well in mink and muskrat trapping where you want to guard a large opening. It may be that I am underestimating this trap since, according to the manufacturers, it is suitable for raccoon, fox, badger, nutria, and woodchuck.

The No. 330 Conibear with its jaw spread of ten by ten inches would make it more suitable for raccoon and fox than the No. 220. However, the 330 size is illegal to use in all but water sets in some states. Also, such trap-wise animals as the fox are not likely to step into a trap which must be partly exposed to function. The No. 330 is *the* trap for beaver and otter, however.

In all fairness, the most versatile trap that can be found for beaver is the large-sized leg-hold trap. The No. 4 double long spring or the wider-jawed under-spring trap will hold a beaver either under the ice or in open water sets and it can be set almost anywhere. However, it does require some skill, and often a bit of luck, to set properly. Conversely, the No. 330 Conibear trap will produce better for the beginner or relatively unskilled trapper since it will compensate for small errors in placement.

The big problem in using leg-hold traps is in setting them at exactly the right depth. A Conibear trap can simply be set where the beaver must swim between the jaws to reach bait, den entrance, or follow a narrow channel.

If you have yet to experiment with the Conibear line of traps, I suggest you do so. They seem especially suited to trapping the water animals—muskrat, beaver, and otter. And they are gaining popularity in trapping mink, marten, and fisher. Should weasel and skunk regain market value, Conibear traps would be a good choice for both.

Generally the Conibear trap is set with the trigger wires facing down, but it will work, often with equal effectiveness, sideways or upside-down. In the case of the No. 110, I spread the trigger wires so that the ends are about two and one-quarter inches apart. This makes it difficult for a mink or muskrat to slip through without tripping the trigger. It is the animal's back, I believe, that most often trips the trigger.

Leg-hold traps

Conventional leg-hold traps (Victor, Oneida, and Newhouse) are designed to catch animals alive, retain them, and leave to the trapper the decision to free or retain the captured animal. In the case of water trapping, leg-hold traps are often set in such a way that a trapped animal will drown soon after capture.

Victor long spring traps are probably the most widely used traps today. They are easy to set and the most economically priced. Single long springs come in sizes 0, 1, and 1½. There is a size 11 which has the same jaw size as the No. 1, but is equipped with double long springs. A young trapper with a dozen No. 1½ single long spring traps can hope to capture such popular furbearers as mink, muskrat, and raccoon. Larger quarry can be taken in No. 2 (fox, raccoon, fisher, opossum, nutria); No. 3 (beaver, coyote, fox, lynx, badger); and No. 4 (otter, beaver, wolf, coyote) in double long spring traps.

Numbers 2, 3, and 4 Victor double long spring traps are equipped with slide (or drowning) locks for aquatic animals. By utilizing the slide lock on a wire, the trapper can insure quick drowning of the trapped animal. Slide locks are incorporated on the chain ring of these traps.

The larger size long spring traps can also be purchased with offset jaws to permit smaller nontarget animals to escape and for wildlife management study.

Figure 12–4 Victor Long Spring traps. (Courtesy of Woodstream Corp.)

No. 0, 1, 1½
Single spring

No. 11, 2, 3, 4
Double spring

156

Figure 12–5 No. 1VG Victor Stop-Loss Trap. (Courtesy
of Woodstream Corp.)

Victor stop-loss traps are designed to eliminate escapes. When an
animal is caught, an auxiliary guard moves high up on its body, holding it
in such a position that it cannot escape. They come in sizes 1 and 1½ and
are primarily for muskrat and mink. These, as well as the No. 110 and
120 Conibear traps, are excellent choices for muskrat.

Because of their light, compact structure, Oneida jump traps are easier
to carry and conceal than long spring traps. They come in sizes 1, 1½, 3,
and 4.

Victor coil-spring traps are my personal favorite. They come in sizes 1,
1½, 2, and 3. They are easy to set and conceal, are exceptionally sturdy,
and have the speed and power to operate effectively in a dirt-hole set.
They also provide for adjustable pan pressure to help prevent the capture
of nontarget animals and insure higher, more secure grips on such escape
artists as the fox and coyote. Ideally, one should have enough pan
pressure that an animal's full weight must be applied before the trap
springs. They are also available with offset jaws.

Newhouse traps have been the favorite of professional trappers since
1848 when Sewell Newhouse first hammered out these traps on a
blacksmith's anvil. They are expensive, but each Newhouse trap is

157

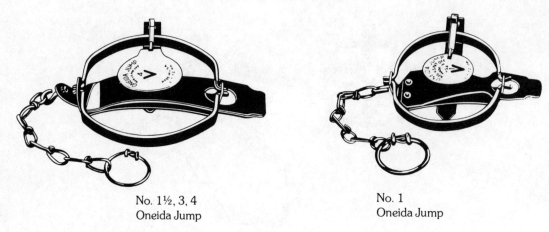

No. 1½, 3, 4
Oneida Jump

No. 1
Oneida Jump

Figure 12–6 Oneida Jump traps. (Courtesy of Woodstream Corp.)

Figure 12–7 Newhouse traps. (Courtesy of Woodstream Corp.)

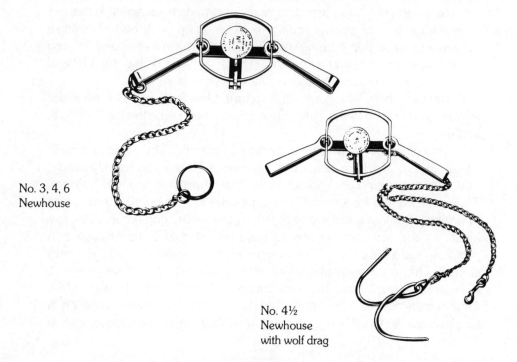

No. 3, 4, 6
Newhouse

No. 4½
Newhouse
with wolf drag

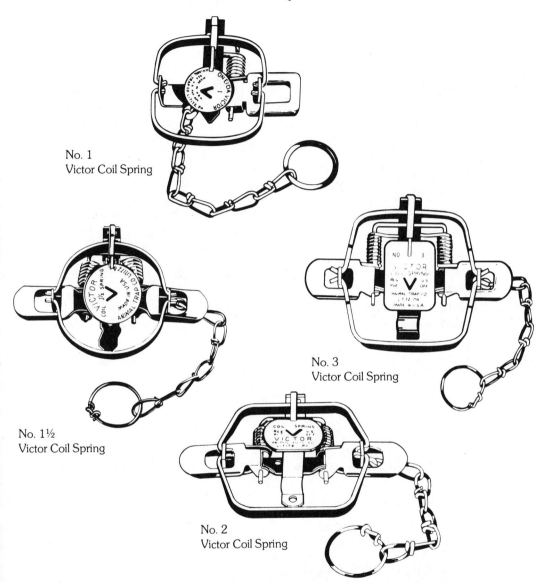

No. 1
Victor Coil Spring

No. 1½
Victor Coil Spring

No. 3
Victor Coil Spring

No. 2
Victor Coil Spring

Figure 12–8 Victor Coil-Spring traps. (Courtesy of Woodstream Corp.)

hand-assembled and tested. All Newhouse traps are equipped with welded, kinkless chains. They are double long spring traps and come in sizes 3, 4, 4½ (for timber wolf, equipped with a drag, weighing eight pounds), and 6 (for bear, furnished with setting clamp and grip, weighing 49½ pounds).

A MODERN TRAPLINE

Snares

Woodstream handles Kleflock and Newhouse snares. All Kleflock snares are made of special rust-proof cable. This cable is lightweight, yet exceptionally strong, and it is not affected by thawing or freezing weather. The Newhouse snare is made of flexible, kink-resisting willow wire with nonslip lock and adjustable end tie.

Type	Length	Type of Animal
Kleflock 0 Standard	6'	rabbit, skunk, woodchuck
Kleflock 2 Standard	6'	coyote, fox, badger, beaver, lynx
Kleflock 0 Swivel	30"	rabbit, skunk, woodchuck
Kleflock 2 Swivel	3'	wolf, fox, coyote, beaver, lynx, badger
Newhouse	8'	wolf, fox, bear

The Raymond Thompson Company has for many years made and sold the Thompson Self-Locking Steel Snare®, a favorite of Canadian and northcountry trappers.

Thompson handles twelve sizes of snares ranging from No. 0–24 inch Swiveled (muskrat, mink, rabbits, and so on) to No. 6–10 foot Swiveled (large bear, including grizzly).

Figure 12–9 Newhouse and Kleflock snares. (Courtesy of Woodstream Corp.)

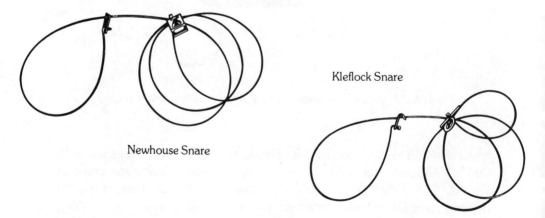

Kleflock Snare

Newhouse Snare

TRAPS AND EQUIPMENT

Equipment

When I was a youngster, about the only equipment I needed was a gunny sack to carry my traps and a hatchet for cutting stakes. We used bark for dyeing traps and carved our stretching boards from scrap wood. You can do the same today if you stick to trapping such common furbearers as mink, muskrat, weasel, skunk, opossum, and raccoon. It's only when you go after the fox and coyote that things get complicated; in fact, most of the accessories that follow are for fox and coyote trapping. Information on stretching boards will be found in Chapter 15; on trap dye and wax, in Chapter 13; and bait and lure, in Chapter 14.

Trap stakes

We made our own stakes for fox and coyote trapping from wood which, unfortunately, sometimes split or broke off. If you must use wood, an excellent stake, usually about 12 inches long for clay soil, longer for sand, can be made from old hardwood flooring. A piece of sheet metal is fitted over the top of the stake and held in place with two nuts and bolts to prevent splitting when pounding on the stake. A final touch is to drive a spike through the stake and sheet metal and then form a loop in the pointed end of the spike. The trap chain can be wired to this loop.

Steel stakes are handier and more commonly used because they won't split or break off and will penetrate frozen and rocky ground. The length of the stake depends on the type of soil you're trapping in. A 12-inch stake might be fine for clay soil, but an 18-inch stake might not hold foxes in very sandy soil. Angle iron is commonly used to make stakes. A hole is drilled near the top of the angle iron and a steel S-hook used for fastening the trap chain.

Since stakes are often buried in the ground or snow, the swivels available on commercial steel stakes are often made inoperable. Thus many trappers make a point of using short chains when staking a trap (with either wooden or steel stakes). This way the animal has little room to jump or twist, and possibly injure itself.

In a recent trapping supplies catalog, steel stakes, already equipped with S-hooks, sell for $10 a dozen, not postpaid. They cost half again as much at a local sporting goods store. Trapping supply houses frequently offer the best buys for the trapper, but you will be wise to order them well in advance of the season.

Treat steel stakes to a logwood bath as you would grapples and traps.

Dirt sifter

This is a handy item for the trapper who covers his traps with dirt. It is a must when making the popular dirt-hole set. The sifter is filled with material dug out of the trap bed and bait hole then, after the trap is set, held above the trap and shaken until the trap is covered. Small stones and twigs, which might lodge in the crotch of the trap jaws and prevent its working, remain in the sifter.

You can buy a dirt sifter from a trapping supply house, but you can easily make your own from scrap wood and one-quarter inch wire mesh available at hardware stores. The wooden framework for the wire mesh should be about nine inches wide, ten inches long, and four inches high.

Pack basket

Carefully woven by hand from selected ratten and seasoned with ash, correctly shaped to fit the back, and equipped with heavy adjustable webbing harness with sponge rubber pads—this pack basket sold by L.L. Bean, Inc. is just one of the commercial brands of pack basket available to the trapper. The pack basket is convenient for carrying bulky, odd shaped items such as steel traps.

Trappers will sometimes modify their pack baskets. Charlie Mechley made a hinged, plywood cover for his. A pouch made of canvas with separate compartments for lure bottles can be hung from the outer rim. Over-sized safety pins can be clipped to the outside for carrying an extra pair of rubber gloves. It is wise to keep bait and lure, and gloves for handling these items, separate from traps, stakes, dirt sifter, and other equipment.

Digging tool

Some kind of digging tool is necessary for making dirt-hole sets, artificial-hole sets, and other dirt sets. A good, heavy duty tool is available from Northwoods Trapline Supplies. It has a six-inch curved blade three inches wide and is tapered and sharp. Its overall length is 22½ inches.

Some trappers prefer to use a conventional garden spade with a somewhat narrowed blade for the initial cutting of sod when making the dirt-hole set. The bait hole is then dug with a smaller hand tool. Northwoods offers a 14-inch-long by three-inch-wide hand digging tool with a 5½-inch cutting edge. A common garden trowel can also be used, but many are not strong enough for rough use.

Small shovels sold as camping tools can be utilized. The folding army entrenching tool would be good if the blade could be narrowed. If it works, that's all that counts.

Gloves

If you do a lot of muskrat, mink, and beaver trapping, a pair of shoulder-length rubber gloves is a good investment. For fox and coyote trapping, wrist length rubber gloves are sufficient. I like those that are lined with flannel and have knit wrists.

For greater comfort and dexterity, you can wear cotton or canvas work gloves when fox and coyote trapping, but you do take the chance of their absorbing foreign odor and they can't be washed off as readily as rubber gloves. Foreign odors can be masked somewhat by rubbing fox or coyote urine into the gloves. Another ploy is to grasp and slide your gloved hand along pine boughs if evergreens grow along your trap line. This is a natural odor to the animals and will not frighten them in small amounts.

Trap covers

Trap covers serve two purposes. They keep dirt from plugging under the trap pan, which could prevent the trap's springing, and wax paper or plastic covers prevent the traps from freezing to the ground or snow. Some trappers will use no covers, especially in the fall before snow and freezing rain. Or, if they use a cover, will use one or two leaves over the pan to keep it clear of dirt.

Paul L. Failor has this to say in his book, *Pennsylvania Trapping and Predator Control Methods:*

> "After the trap is set and well bedded you are ready for the pan cover, if you choose to use it. Pan covers are made of canvas, metal fly screen, cloth, paper, etc., cut slightly smaller than the inside dimensions of the trap jaws. Because they are unnecessary and also a potential carrier of human odor, they are not recommended. If the trap is set as previously suggested, on a 'hair edge,' you will do much better to forget about the pan cover."

Failor makes a good point. Nevertheless, some of the best fox and coyote trappers use canvas trap covers in the fall and wax paper in the winter. Because wax paper will sometimes make a crackling sound when stepped on, it should first be crumpled, unrolled, and recrumpled several times. Canvas covers should be washed and allowed to "air" from a clothesline for a week or so before being used.

163

Drags

Commercially made steel drags (grapples) are available and are considered superior to stakes by many coyote and wolf trappers, since these animals are powerful and sometimes difficult to hold in a solidly staked trap. The drag is a two-pronged affair that looks like two giant fishhooks back to back. It works best when coupled to a couple of feet of extension chain that is wired or linked to the end of the trap chain. The drag and extension chain are buried beneath the trap and, when a coyote or wolf is caught, the animal is able to leave the set location but becomes entangled upon entering thick cover.

A coyote or wolf is a powerful animal, but it cannot exert its full strength against a drag as it can against a solidly staked trap. The drag continually becomes snagged, unsnagged, then resnagged again, although it is usually firmly hung up by the time the trapper arrives. Coyote and wolf grapples are generally about nine inches long by seven inches wide and made of three-eighths inch or better steel. They are also occasionally used by fox and bobcat trappers, particularly in the winter months when it is not easy to pound a stake into the ground. Drags should be dyed with logwood along with the traps.

Trap covering material

Dry dirt, grass clippings, sawdust, and ashes all are handy items on the trapline. I'm sure that countless numbers of trappers have gotten along quite nicely without bothering to collect these items during the summer months for use on the fall and winter trapline. Nevertheless, they are nice to have when you need them and it doesn't take much time to accumulate enough for a trapping season.

Dry dirt is very handy for trap covering in dirt-hole sets once the ground is frozen or the dirt at the site is wet and subject to freezing. Dig several pails of dirt during a summer dry spell and dry the dirt even more by spreading it out on a hard surface. A large plywood panel that was no longer much good did the trick for us. Do this in an open, sunlit spot. Turn the dirt occasionally with a shovel. Once it is dry, store it in clean pails in a sheltered spot. We had to cover ours to keep neighborhood cats from using the dirt for their toilet. I've read that anthill material makes good winter trap covering because the material has a light, wax-like coating, but I've never tried it.

Grass clippings are nice to have for dry land sets made for mink. Often the natural vegetation at the set location is heavy and coarse and may

164

plug the action of the trap if used for trap covering. I got all we needed one day by raking the grass clippings into piles after I cut the lawn. After several days of warm, sunny weather and occasionally turning the piles, the clippings were converted into hay. I stored it in plastic garbage bags. Admittedly I did not put it to much use, although it came in handy on a couple of occasions when I made mink and raccoon sets near the roadside. One trapper I met likes to use grass clippings to cover traps set for muskrat on logs and floating raft sets.

Sawdust is often easy to get and should be dried in the same manner as dirt or grass clippings. It is a natural covering for traps set in hollow logs and stumps.

Wood ash is saved by some trappers to use in campfire sets for fox. Foxes often scratch around old campfires in secluded or otherwise closed for the season campgrounds in search of food. Wood ash is a natural covering for this set. Bits of cheese or bacon make good bait. Because wood ash is so light, traps can be concealed under two or three inches of it. I've never used this set, but it was an old favorite of Charlie Mechleys.

Miscellaneous items

Among the items sometimes available through trapping supply houses are:

1. Springs—can be fitted under the old spring of a long spring trap to add to its speed and holding power.
2. Extension chains—for trap chains.
3. S-hooks—for fastening drags or trap stakes to trap chains.
4. Rubber crawfish—to clip to the pan of the trap to lure mink and raccoon.
5. Push-pins—for attaching all pelts smaller than beaver and otter to wooden stretchers. These can be used over and over again and require no hammer, but they must be used with stretchers made from soft wood.
6. Setting tools—for Conibear traps and long spring traps.
7. Catching tool—combines a length of hollow pipe, a snare, and a trigger arrangement for releasing unwanted animals from traps.
8. Trap tags—for areas where traps must be marked with the owner's name and address.
9. Tail stripper—for removing tail bones from raccoon, fox, skunk, mink, and so on.
10. Fur drying frames and fleshing tools.

13
Dyeing
and Waxing Traps

Dyeing traps either with commercial logwood crystals or native bark replaces the odor of steel with a natural woodsy odor, helps prevent rusting, and makes the traps easier to conceal by giving them a dark hue. Oddly, traps must be rusty before they can be treated to prevent rust. Smooth shiny steel will not take on a good color. If you've just bought new steel traps and trapping season is only a week away, you may as well forget about dyeing the traps until next year since it takes several weeks to develop a coat of rust. If your quarry is muskrat, it won't make much difference. Muskrat, raccoon, opossum, weasel, and skunk are not deterred by a slight odor of steel, oil, or rust, nor are they alarmed by a shiny trap. Even mink and otter can be taken in untreated traps if water sets are used. It is the trapping of fox or coyote for which traps must be treated. But be sure to dye those new traps the following year, because this treatment will add to the life of the traps. Even when they've been dyed once, it is usually necessary to repeat the treatment yearly.

New traps have a coating of oil to prevent rust. You want to first remove this oil so the traps will rust and take a coating of dye. This is accomplished by boiling the traps in a tub of water. Some trappers add lye to the water to help remove the oil. This is a caustic substance, so use it with care. (You *can* get by without it.)

166

Figure 13–1 Traps need to be rusty to take a good coating of dye. I hastened the process by putting these in water and mud.

Boiling traps is an outside job. If you don't have an outside fireplace, improvise one by piling some flat stones into a U shape about two feet high. Place several iron bars across the walls to support your tub of water. We happened to have some concrete building blocks and set two pairs of these on end with iron bars across the ends. I bought a barrel at a garage sale to hold the traps for boiling. We left this in position all through the trapping season, and it came in handy when, later in the season, I wanted to redye the traps I was using for coyotes.

After the traps have boiled a short time, a film of oil will be seen on the surface. Either pour this off the top, or add more water to the tub or barrel so that it overflows and the oil on the surface runs out with the water. The traps can then be hung outside to take on a coating of rust.

This treatment can be skipped if the traps are already rusty or you have bought traps well enough in advance of the trapping season that they will take on rust from being outside over a long period of time. Some trappers will submerge their traps in a lake or swamp for a week or so and then hang them out in the weather.

To dye traps once they have a coating of rust (or to redye them if they have been dyed before), boil the traps in a tub of water with either commercial logwood crystals or native bark. We used logwood crystals from Northwoods Trapline Supplies, following the manufacturer's directions for use. The traps are slowly simmered in the brew for about 10 minutes, allowed to sit for 30, and then brought to a slow simmer again.

I believe the price of the logwood crystals was $2.50 per package. One package will dye about three dozen traps.

It is possible to make your own dye from native bark that is high in tannic acid, such as maple, oak, and walnut. Many trappers use the walnuts themselves, collecting them hull and all, as they fall to the ground. They can be used either green or when they turn black. Use a pail of these to a barrel of water. It makes a potent solution.

As far as I'm concerned, waxing traps is more hazardous than it is worth. But for those who choose to go on to the waxing process, remove traps from the water and allow them to dry completely. This is important, as wet traps or traps that are hotter than the wax (such as those just lifted from a boiling wood dye solution) will not take a good coating of wax. When the traps are perfectly dry, place a bucket of commercial trap wax over a small fire and heat it until the wax is melted and smoking hot. There must be enough wax to cover a trap completely. Now dip each trap into the wax. Leave the trap in the wax solution a minimum of one minute to be certain that each trap reaches the same temperature as the wax. Pull out the trap, shake off the excess wax, and hang it in an airy shed or garage.

Figure 13–2 Dyeing traps is an outdoor job. It is especially necessary for trapping fox and coyote.

14
Bait
and Lure

Bait and lure are very important parts of a fox and coyote trapper's equipment. They are also useful in trapping raccoon, skunk, opossum, marten, wolverine, weasel, badger, bobcat, and fisher. Mink, muskrat, beaver, and otter can also be taken with bait and lure, but these animals, as well as raccoon, are often trapped successfully without bait or lure by setting traps where the animals enter and exit the water.

Although they can produce results separately, bait and lure are usually used in conjunction. Young trappers sometimes pin all their hopes on the power of lures to attract fur animals to their sets. Lures are helpful if properly used, but they will not take the place of proper baits and care and skill in making sets. It is also well to remember that rain and snow may obliterate lure but the trap and the bait will still be on the job.

Lure is a valuable asset to any trapline, but it will not perform miracles. If it's made right, it will draw the desired animal in close to your set, and then it all depends on your skill as a trapper. The best set is still one that is attractive to the desired animal, regardless of whether bait and lure are used.

A few trappers make their own lure, but home lure-making is complicated, messy, and more often than not the amateur lure-maker will end up chasing away more furbearers than he lures in. Commercial lures, available for everything from bears through housemice, are reasonably priced and well worth it. I'll deal here with the more popular animals and the use of bait and lure in taking them.

Fox

Of all the baits and lures sold commercially, more are made for taking fox than any other animal. This is especially true of lures, since most trappers are able to supply their own bait. Glancing through the trapping supply catalog offered by S. Stanley Hawbaker & Sons, one finds over fifteen lures for fox.

Fox lure is usually made from the glands, anus, and urine of the animal. It may also contain glands and parts from other animals. The lures sell for about $2.50 for a one-ounce bottle. Twenty-five foxes can easily be taken with a single ounce of good lure. Just a few drops of lure are used with the dirt-hole set.

Urine, which runs about $6 per pint, is also used but in more generous amounts. Urine is a suspicion remover. Good fox urine is one of the most important tools of the trapping trade. It will call foxes from a greater distance than any other known substance. It is the basic ingredient in the compounding of many different fox lures—an item that can make the difference between just a fair catch and a good or excellent catch. Few foxes can resist the temptation to investigate a set where a good grade of urine has been liberally used.

Tainted bait for fox

Bait for foxes can be made from woodchuck, porcupine, prairie dog, rock chuck, skunk, legally taken muskrat, beaver, or rabbit. Generally such bait is cut into two-inch square cubes and allowed to become slightly tainted. Incidentally, there are probably many, many other kinds of animals the flesh of which would be attractive to foxes. It is hard to come by nowadays, but hog lard cracklings are an old and still reliable bait. My friend Charlie Mechley swears by it. In fact, he finds the cracklings, which are not unlike crispy pieces of bacon, to be excellent trail food.

Woodchuck makes a good bait and is used by many fox trappers in the East because it is abundant, good-sized, and unprotected in most states. Farmers are often glad to have their fields rid of them. If you plan to start trapping foxes around November 1, you'll want to shoot several woodchucks in late September or early October. Put each into a heavy

171

paper bag immediately. This will prevent flies from landing on the carcasses, thereby keeping maggots out of your bait jar.

After the sun goes down and the flies are out of the picture, take the woodchucks from the bag, remove the entrails, and with your hatchet cut the carcass into two-inch-square cubes. It is not necessary to skin the animal. Use all but the entrails, feet, and tail. Put the cubes into a clean fruit jar. If you can get them, plastic jars would be better. Screw the lid down lightly so gases can escape. Bury the jar under a few inches of dirt in a cool, shaded spot. In a week or so it will be tainted and ready to use. You'll want to start putting it out before the trapping season to get the foxes used to coming to your sets.

By adding preservative to it, tainted bait can be prepared at any time and kept indefinitely. When "canning" bait like this, it is best to skin the animal and cut the meat from the bones. Ethylene glycol, a colorless, liquid that is the main ingredient in automobile antifreeze, is used as a preservative. Because it has a tendency to kill the odor of tainted bait, your bait must be more tainted than usual. Instead of burying the bait I find it more convenient to keep it in a shed where I can keep track of the tainting process by occasionally smelling the contents. When it smells tainted, I let it set for another week and then add enough ethylene glycol to completely cover the bait. You don't need much, maybe two ounces, because the deboned meat compacts.

Once a day I stir the contents slightly to be sure the preservative reaches all the bait. Once the bait is preserved, which may take a week or more, the cover can be screwed down tightly. A test you can make is to have the cover tight for half a day and then slowly loosen the cover. If you hear gas escaping, it is not fully preserved.

We were given several jars of bait last fall that were preserved with ethylene glycol and it really did the job. It was made from the flesh of domestic rabbit and was very effective for fox, coyote, and raccoon. I made some this spring using the flesh of spring-trapped beaver.

If you are unable to get ethylene glycol, I have seen bait preservative sold in at least one sporting goods store. The manufacturer was O. L. Butcher, a time-honored name in trapping supplies.

I recently contacted the Olin Chemical Company in New Haven, Connecticut, and told them of using ethylene glycol as a bait preservative and as antifreeze for winter trapping. Their technical representative suggested substituting propylene glycol, which is less toxic than ethylene glycol. This product, I was told, would be available in small quantities from most any chemical supply company (see your yellow pages).

Tainted bait can be *too* rotten. This is particularly a problem during fall when various fruits are still available and the foxes are taking only a limited amount of flesh. If the bait is too rotten the fox may roll in it, and this almost always results in a sprung trap rather than a trapped fox.

Coyote

Baits, lures, and sets that take foxes will also take coyotes. Because of this it pays to use fox lure and uring at dirt-hole sets when trapping in spots where the two animals sometimes overlap. Fox lure is used because it will lure foxes and yet not discourage coyotes who have no fear of foxes. Foxes, on the other hand, are deathly afraid of coyotes and may not approach a set if they smell coyote lure or urine.

When coyotes are the main quarry, however, coyote lure and urine are preferred. Tainted bait, such as that used in fox trapping, is also used. Lures for coyote rank second in number to those sold for fox.

Mink

Lure manufacturers usually handle one or two kinds of mink lure as well as mink urine. Bait is supplied by the trapper, usually small pieces of fish, muskrat flesh, or the intestines of small birds and animals. Chunks of eel are used by trappers in the East. Canned sardines and similar fare give off a strong odor and are often effective. Trappers who rely heavily on bait use the pocket set a lot. Along a soft grassy bank, they part the overhanging grass and dig a hole in the bank about six inches deep just above the level of the water. Bait is placed in the hole and lure and urine may be added. Fish oil is another attraction.

Probably more mink are taken in blind sets than any other. Bait and lure are never used with a blind set, but urine can be. Mink urine is a real suspicion remover. Always try to place it in a sheltered spot where it will not be washed away by rain or snow.

Mink can be trapped successfully without bait, lure or urine, but in the right circumstances, a touch of either can put a mink in your trap that might otherwise have been missed.

Raccoon

While raccoon can be trapped quite successfully in blind sets, such as where they enter or exit the water or walk through a culvert, bait can markedly improve your catch. Especially in the fall, raccoon seem determined to stuff themselves at every opportunity. We found that the same bait of tainted wild and domestic rabbit used for fox and coyote was equally attractive to raccoon, but something fishy smelling is even better.

Fish oil goes well with raccoon sets. Sardines, herring, and similar fare is excellent. Sometimes the trapper can catch large numbers of rough fish such as carp and suckers. Chunks of these either fresh or slightly tainted are good.

Because the raccoon is omnivorous, all manner of baits will lure him, including sweet baits like honey, jam, and peanut butter. Most of the lures sold for raccoon trapping are sweet-smelling. Oil of anise, available at drugstores, is good. Once it catches wind of your bait, a raccoon is almost sure to investigate.

Muskrat

Muskrats are caught by the thousands each year in blind sets—places where the animals have been entering or exiting the water, crawling onto a partly submerged log or a stone protruding above the level of the water, as well as in their underwater burrows and houses or feeder stations. But they also can be taken with the use of lure and bait. Bait can be apple, carrot, parsnip, green turnip tops, potatoes, corn, and even the flesh of another muskrat.

You can add to the attractiveness of bait with sweet-smelling lure. Oil of anise is good, as are any of the commercial lures.

Carrion and fish oil

Carrion, such as a dead deer, is a very attractive lure for wolf, coyote, fox, bobcat, and fisher during the winter months when the snow lies deep and food is scarce. Often carrion can be found by watching for the activity of ravens, crows, and buzzards.

Fish oil is not only an important part of many lure formulas, but a very effective "caller" when used alone. You can easily prepare your own.

Cut suckers, carp, eels, or any fatty fish into chunks and put them into a heavy glass gallon jar. Lay a flat piece of glass over the top, permitting the gases to escape and at the same time preventing flies from entering the jar. Keep the jar in full sun at all times and away from cats and dogs. A good place for the fish oil jar is on top of the roof of a small building.

As the solids deteriorate, the oil will begin to appear on the surface. After several weeks of "sun rendering" several inches of clear yellow to amber colored oil will have risen to the top.

Pour or siphon off the oil into a clean bottle. Put your gallon jar back in the sun. It is quite likely that several more ounces will be rendered within a few weeks.

15

Handling
Your Furs

The trapper has a number of options open to him when handling furs. He can bring in the animals he catches on a regular basis, say every week or so, and sell them to the fur buyer as is, leaving to the fur buyer the job of skinning, fleshing, and drying the pelts. Regular trips to the buyer are not necessary when temperatures are below freezing, as animals can be kept frozen in a garage, shed, or barn without spoilage. I've seen winter catches of fox, coyote, bobcat, and fisher brought in frozen, and occasionally I've brought in the whole animal when I've been in a hurry for extra cash. In cold climates it may take three or four days to thaw a coyote found frozen in a trap or snare and another week to dry the pelt on a stretching board. Obviously the buyer will have to deduct the cost of what he pays to have the animals skinned, fleshed, and dried. This may not be as much as you think. Our local buyer was only deducting $2.00 for such difficult-to-handle animals as raccoon, beaver, and otter during the 1978 to 1979 season.

Another option is to skin your catch but leave the fleshing and drying to the buyer. I did this when I trapped beaver during our spring season. I was able to bring the pelts in as fequently as I caught them because we have a fur buyer in the community where I live.

If I'd wanted to keep the skinned but undried pelts until the end of the

175

season and the weather was warm, I would have had to freeze the pelts, which is another option open to the trapper. By freezing the skinned but green (undried) pelts, there is no danger of their spoiling; 24 hours before they are to be sold, the pelts can be thawed. This is necessary so that the buyer can closely examine the pelts. Before freezing, be sure that the fur is dry and free of mud and burrs, then roll the pelt into a ball, fur side out. Put the fur into a sealable plastic bag. I'll sometimes put the plastic bag into a brown paper bag for additional protection, fold it, tie it securely with string, and then store it in a deep freeze.

The final option is to do one's own skinning, fleshing, and drying. Normally, this brings the optimum prices for your pelts. I say normally because if you sell your furs when the top price for large raccoon, say, is $40 skinned, fleshed, and dried, and then two weeks later the price for large raccoon rises to $55, someone who has not bothered to even skin his catch is going to get more money than you did. So even with well-handled pelts it pays to know when to sell. (I'll have more to say about that in Chapter 16.)

Without a good fleshing beam, a decent fleshing tool, and the experience of handling many thousands of pelts, the trapper can spend many hours fleshing a single beaver pelt. An experienced fur handler can do the job in minutes. However, it isn't pointless for the trapper to do the complete job of skinning, fleshing and drying his own pelts.

Animals such as mink, muskrat, fox, and coyote have little excess flesh on the hide and it is easily removed with a low-priced or makeshift tool. Many muskrat pelts have been fleshed with a kitchen spoon. The pelts are easily dried on homemade or commercial stretchers. Even the difficult beaver, raccoon, and otter are not too much trouble for many trappers. In fact, the careful skinning, fleshing, and drying of the pelts of the animals that one has caught is often a matter of pride. We did a complete job on everything we caught, with the exception of spring-caught beaver and a few winter-caught fox and coyote.

It has its practical advantages, too. If you do not have a freezer at your disposal or do not care to store pelts in a home freezer during warm autumn or spring days, the only other recourse is to do the complete job of skinning, fleshing, and drying. And you have little choice if you plan to ship your furs to a buyer or auction in another state.

Many state trapper's associations hold fur sales for their members. Trappers who take the trouble to skin, flesh, and dry their pelts usually get the top prices. No amount of handling care will salvage an unprime or damaged pelt, but doing the complete job never hurts when done right and can bring in extra dollars.

HANDLING YOUR FURS

Skinning

I doubt it is possible to describe in print or pictures the process of skinning an animal, at least not well enough to get the complete novice started. You have to see it done, at least once, and even then it takes a number of trapping seasons to become proficient at it. What I hope to do here is to give some general advice; then I suggest you make an effort to watch the skinning job done by someone hired by a fur buyer. These persons have skinned hundreds, possibly thousands, of different animals and they invariably have a system. Each beaver, for instance, will be handled in exactly the same way. When you watch the job done by one of these pros, you can be reasonably certain that the steps taken are the shortest and the best for skinning that animal.

You do have one advantage over the professional skinner; you have the chance to skin an animal while it is still warm. Raccoon, fox, and coyote are usually alive in the trap. If you skin the animal within an hour or so of its death, it will still be warm and the pelt will come off much more easily.

All furs should be dry and brushed free of mud, briars, and burrs before skinning. To dry a wet animal, hang by its front feet or head. If hung by the tail or hind legs, moisture will penetrate deeper into the fur. In the case of an animal skinned in the field, these steps can be taken later at home. Be sure the fur is dry before putting a pelt on a stretching board.

Mink and raccoon tails should be opened on the underside after skinning. This is done by inserting an umbrella rib in the tail with the groove of the rib facing the underside of the tail. Place the point of a sharp knife in the groove and slide it down the groove to the end of the tail. This is important to do on mink and raccoon since the hide is quite oily inside the tail. I rarely bother with this on fox or coyote, although I'll open the underside of the tail for the first three or four inches with my knife during the skinning process to make removal of the tail bone easier.

All animals should be case-skinned with the exception of beaver and badger. This means that the pelt should be removed as you would a pullover sweater, after first making a cut from one hind foot to the base of the tail and on to the other hind foot (a pinch of fur is usually left around the anus).

The beaver pelt is removed by cutting up the belly from the tail to the lower jaw and taking it off as you would a coat. Circular cuts are made around each foot and the tail. In fact, the feet should be removed on beaver to aid in removing the pelt.

Don't worry about leaving globs of meat on a beaver pelt. This is hard

177

to avoid around the hind legs and front shoulders. If you try to skin these areas too cleanly you may cut the pelt. Be very careful along the lower spine. The hide holds tight and you have to use a knife every inch of the way.

Animals are easier to skin when you hang them during skinning by a hind foot. An exception is the beaver. Beaver can be handled on the ground or on a table top with the animal on its back.

The pelt is difficult to work loose around a fox or coyotes forelegs. You can make it easier on yourself by making a slit in the backside of each foreleg from the ankle to the leg joint.

Fleshing

Beaver, raccoon, otter, skunk, and opossum all require a lot of fleshing and the job is best done on some kind of fleshing beam. When we removed a tree from our yard I cut a crotch of the tree to use as a fleshing beam (see Figure 15-1). A similar beam could be made from a log with one end propped off the ground around waist level. The surface must be smooth or it could result in cuts in the hide when fleshing. I considered nailing a piece of sheet metal over our beam, but it wasn't necessary.

With this kind of fleshing beam, the hide is draped over the beam with one end held in place by leaning one's stomach against the hide. A two-handled fleshing tool is pressed down and away from one's self. This is the method used by our local fur buyer.

We bought a moderately priced fleshing tool from a trapper's supply house for around $5. I've seen the same kind in a number of trapping supply catalogs. I don't recommend this tool—it's too small and the flimsy handles kept falling off. As it was, we made do, and we fleshed many a fatty raccoon pelt.

If no fleshing beam is available, mink, muskrat, fox, coyote, and raccoon can all be fleshed on a wooden stretching board.

Stretching and drying

Pelts should be dried on either commercial wire stretchers or homemade wooden stretchers. Actually, wooden stretchers can also be bought commercially. Northwoods Trapline and Hunting Supplies' catalog, advertises wooden stretchers for fox, raccoon, and mink. The mink boards are available in three sizes: No. 1 for female mink, No. 2 for male mink, and No. 3 for male jumbo mink.

HANDLING YOUR FURS

Except for buying a dozen wire stretchers for muskrat, I made my own stretching boards using an old wire fox and raccoon stretcher as a model for some, and a couple of different-sized commercial wooden mink stretchers as models for others. I used a mink board to fashion two stretching boards for otter. The shape is identical, only the otter board is much longer and wider.

I made several adjustable stretching boards for raccoon. Raccoons come in many sizes and the adjustable stretchers came in handy.

Unless you have access to free wood such as sometimes found in dumps, abandoned buildings, or whatever, it will be wise to buy the wire commercial stretcher. They do an excellent job of drying pelts and pelts tend to dry faster on them since there is more air circulation. Pelts, I might

Figure 15–1 Using a fleshing beam made from the crotch of a tree.

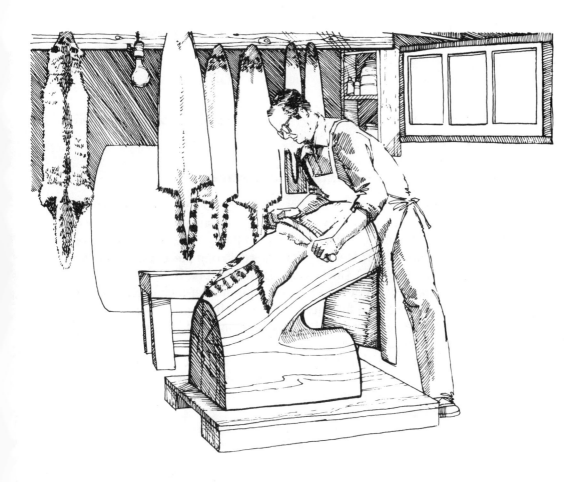

Newhouse   Quick Dry

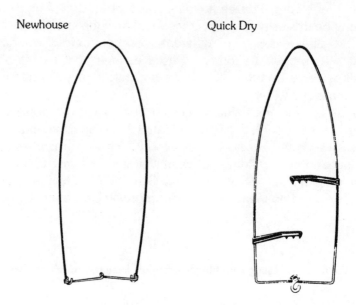

**Figure 15–2 Newhouse® and Quick-Dry® fur drying frames.
(Courtesy of Woodstream Corp.)**

add, are not really stretched. They are simply pulled snug then pinned, nailed, or fastened.

Adjustable stretchers

Because raccoons come in all sizes it is handy to have a few adjustable stretchers. The main ingredient needed to make such a stretcher is scrap wood one-half to one-inch thick and at least three inches wide. You need two pieces of scrap four feet long for the sides, one piece a foot long for the base, and one piece 18 inches long for the tail board.

Other materials needed are three one-quarter-inch bolts (length depending on the actual thickness of the wood), three one-quarter-inch wing nuts, six flat washers, and a large finishing nail. The tools needed are a plane, a drill, and a jigsaw.

To get the desired shape, take a commercial wire raccoon stretcher and lay one side of it on one of the four-foot-long pieces. Use a pencil to trace the outer edge of the wire stretcher. Repeat this with the other four-foot section.

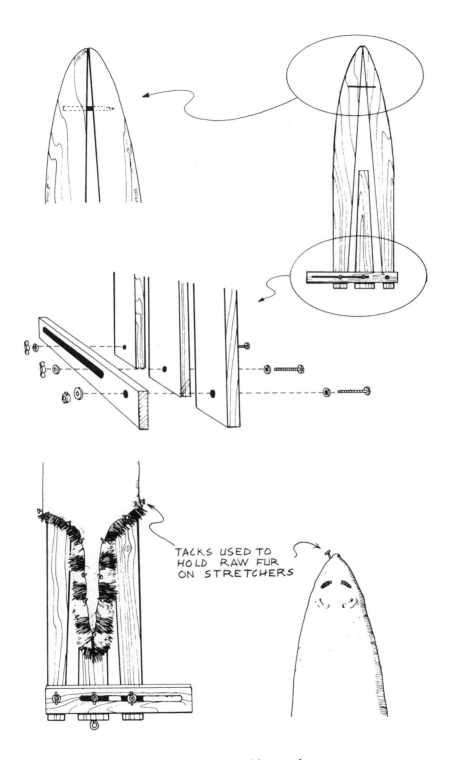

TACKS USED TO
HOLD RAW FUR
ON STRETCHERS

Figure 15–3 Adjustable stretcher.

181

Figure 15–4 Front and rear view of the adjustable raccoon stretching board.

Because wire stretchers bulge in the middle, you may wish to squeeze the stretcher in the middle and hold it in place with tape before tracing an outline. I did this with a couple of the stretchers I made and it made them more suitable for the occasional red fox pelt I stretched on them. It wasn't absolutely necessary for raccoon, which tend to bulge a little in the middle, anyway.

Use a jigsaw or sabre saw to cut the two four-foot pieces to shape. Use a plane or draw knife to round the outer edges. If you like, you can sand the outer edges smooth.

Next, in the narrow flat edge opposite the planed, rounded edge, drill a one-eighth-inch hole near the nose end about five inches from the end. Locate the identical point in the other piece and drill another one-eighth-inch hole. Eventually, a finishing nail with the head cut off will be wedged in these two holes. (See Figure 15-3, top.)

Next drill a one-quarter-inch hole at the bottom of each four-foot piece. These are drilled into the face of the wood, as opposed to the eighth-inch holes that were drilled into the edge. Drill a similar hole near the bottom of the tail board.

The base piece for the adjustable stretcher is a piece of scrap wood one-foot long and two-to three-inches wide. Drill a one-quarter-inch hole one inch from each end. Drill a third quarter-inch hole five inches from one end. With a jigsaw, cut a one-quarter-inch slot from this third hole to the end hole farthest from it. See Figure 15-3 for an illustration of this.

To assemble the stretcher, take one of the side pieces and bolt it to the single hole in the base piece with one of the bolts and wing nuts. Be sure to place a flat washer on each side of the bolt next to the wood. Now bolt the second side of the bolt next to the wood. Now bolt the second side piece through the base's slot.

Take the finishing nail and wedge it in the one-eighth-inch holes drilled in the nose ends of the side pieces, shown in Figure 15-3, top. Adjustments may have to be made so the sides of the pieces fit together at the end. Now position the tail board between the two side pieces and bolt it to the base slot.

Put a raccoon pelt on the stretcher by loosening the wing nuts on the side piece and tail board. Slip the pelt over the stretcher. (See Figure 15-3B.) Tack the tail to the tail board, then tack the legs down on the side pieces. Now pull the loose side piece along the slot until the pelt is taut. Tighten the bolt. Center the tail board between the side pieces and tighten it. The pelt is now stretched.

The dried pelt is easily removed by pulling out the tacks, loosening the bolts, and sliding the side pieces together.

183

Wooden stretching boards

Looking from left to right at our stretching boards in Figure 15-5, the tiny board in the upper left is a weasel board. This was a novelty item since there presently is no market for weasel, or ermine. Next to it is a commercial wire stretcher suitable for fox or small raccoon. To the right of the wire stretcher are two commercially made mink boards. The larger one on the left is $5/16$ inch thick, $35\frac{1}{2}$ inches long, and tapers from $5\frac{1}{4}$

Figure 15–5 Some of the stretching boards we used while operating a fulltime trapline.

inches at the base to 3¼ inches at the shoulder. Shoulder measurement is taken 8 inches from the nose.

The smaller mink board is ⁵/₁₆ inch thick, 35½ inches long, and tapers from 3⅞ inches at the base to 26 inches at the shoulder. Shoulder measurement is taken 8 inches from the nose.

Note that the top of each mink board is well rounded rather than coming to a sharp point. The larger board handled adult male and female mink nicely. The smaller board was good for young mink and small females. Some of the young mink fit on the larger board, but if we got extra length putting them on the smaller board, we did so. Our local fur buyer seemed more impressed with length than width.

The next stretcher is a commercial wire model used for muskrat. Next to it is a wooden muskrat stretcher made from scrap wood. I won't give the dimensions of it because I'd rather you used a commercial wire stretcher as a model if you plan to make your own wooden boards. Muskrat boards should not be more than five-sixteenths-inch thick. Wooden boards should not bulge in the sides as do the wire commercial kind (this bulge straightens when a pelt is in place).

The large adjustable stretcher shown in the lower left of the photo was meant for coyote, but it did not work out. It was so tight in the shoulder area when a pelt was in place that we couldn't stretch the body area taut. It was just right, however, for jumbo-sized raccoon. The smaller adjustable board is the model described earlier for raccoon.

The third board from the lower left is for large raccoon and is ¾ inch thick, 48 inches long, and is 10 inches wide at the base and stays at that width until roughly 17 inches from the nose, at which point it tapers to the nose.

The fourth board from the lower left is for red fox. It is ¾ inch thick, 46¾ inches long, and tapers from 10 inches at the base to 6¾ inches at the shoulder. Shoulder measurement is taken 12 inches from the nose. This board can be a little tight in the shoulder area. You might want to taper to 6 inches at the shoulder or use a thinner board.

The fifth board from the lower left is for otter. It proved too short and I had to add more board to the base. As shown, the board is ¾ inch thick, 49½ inches long, and tapers from 9 inches at the base to 6⅜ inches at the shoulder. Shoulder measurement is taken 12 inches from the nose. I had to add 15 inches to this board, so you really want a board around 72 inches long to be on the safe side. The base will be wider than 9 inches.

The sixth board from the lower left is for large fisher and is ¾ inch thick, 47 inches long, and tapers from 7 inches at the base to 5¾ inches at the shoulder. Shoulder measurement is taken 12 inches from the nose.

The big squarish board leaning against the tree is for beaver and is roughly three feet wide by three and one-half feet high. I painted in the approximate shape of a beaver hide as a guide. A pelt can be stretched on both sides.

Wooden stretching boards for skunk should be 30 inches long, one-half inch thick, 8 inches wide at the base, and 7 inches at the shoulder. Those for the smaller spotted skunk should be 24 inches long, 5½ inches wide at the base, and 5 inches at the shoulder.

Stretching boards for opossum should be 30 inches in length, one-half inch thick, 8 inches at the base, and 7 inches at the shoulder.

Stretching boards for marten should be 36 inches long, a little over 4 inches wide at the base and 3½ inches at the shoulder.

Wolverine are usually skinned open and nailed flat to a board flesh side up.

Badger furs are handled as open pelts and are stretched square. The badger is normally a fatty animal and although they are not hard to skin, they do require a lot of fleshing to produce a top quality pelt.

We kept a small fan going in the basement when we kept our furs and it really helped in the drying process. One night I put three mink on stretchers and the next day I could have taken the smallest one off. The flesh side already felt paperlike. The temperature was between 55 and 60 degrees F, which is about right.

Mink, muskrat, raccoon, otter, skunk, weasel, and opossum are put on drying boards flesh side out and removed when the flesh is dry and paperlike to the touch. Extremely fatty animals such as raccoon never do seem to reach this stage, but are usually dry enough after one to two weeks on a drying board.

Because pelts will shrink during the drying process, it is wise to use an insert. This is a slim, well-sanded stick of wood that is inserted under the belly side of the pelt between the board and the pelt. When the insert is removed, there will be enough slack in the pelt to afford easy removal from the drying board. An insert for mink might be one-half-inch thick by one inch wide at the base by two and one-half feet long, tapering to a point at the end. Inserts are not required when using an adjustable stretcher or wire commerical stretcher.

Fox, coyote, and bobcat pelts were first put on a stretching board flesh side out and after one night were turned and the drying process completed with the fur side out. I didn't dare have the fan blowing on a fox pelt that first night for fear the flesh side would get too dry and I would have difficulty in turning the hide. Fox have a particularly thin hide.

Should one get too dry to turn, wrap the hide in wet burlap until it is soft enough to turn.

When drying on a wooden stretcher, we used an insert. After five or six days the fox, coyote, or bobcat pelt would be removed and the drying process completed off the board. This was to allow better air circulation to reach the flesh which, as I've already pointed out, is on the inside on fox, coyote, and bobcat. Lynx are handled in the same manner. Fisher and marten can be handled either flesh side out or in.

Small pelts are usually held in place on wooden stretchers with pins or small tacks. Small finishing nails may be used for larger pelts such as fox and raccoon. The tails should be split and nailed flat on mink, raccoon, otter, and skunk.

When in doubt about how pelts should be handled, talk with the nearest fur buyer. It is to his advantage that you bring in well-handled pelts.

16

Selling Your Furs

A few years back I drove to a fur buyer with a coyote I'd caught in one of my snares that morning. This was before the price on coyote began to soar. The coyote was frozen harder than the iron ore country in which I'd caught it. I would have preferred to have taken the time to thaw, skin, flesh, and dry the pelt, but I needed some extra money right away.

There were two fur buyers in the community I was heading for and I had done little business with either. The one buyer was well established and, I was told, really knew fur. I had planned to sell the coyote to him, but he was closed that day so I went to the other buyer. After much criticism of the coyote's dark coloration (light-colored coyotes are still preferred), he offered me $25. I was so desperate for money that I almost took it, but I vaguely remembered that coyotes sold for about $25 a year or two before. They should be worth more as everything else was going up in price.

"Maybe I'll take this one home and stretch it," I said, and left.

The next morning I sold the coyote to the established buyer for $45, almost double what the first buyer had offered. I've never gone back to that first buyer. Obviously he'd taken the chance that I was not an experienced trapper and didn't know what the coyote was worth. And he almost got me.

The very best information you can have at your disposal when you go in to sell furs is what those furs are currently selling for. Call every trapper you know and a few you don't know and find out if they've sold any furs recently. Now I am not good at wheeling and dealing. It is embarrassing for me to walk out on a buyer after he has spent considerable time grading my furs. But if I know that adult male mink are selling for $28 and someone offers me $22, I get angry enough to do just that.

Sometimes I'm wrong. An experienced fur buyer will spot flaws that I never notice. The strange part is that even though I'm wrong and the furs are worth exactly what I've been offered, I may get more money from another buyer. Not all buyers have years of experience behind them, and they may not notice the flaws spotted by the experienced buyer, or if they do may take a chance that they can slip the damaged pelts past the New York buyers.

Here is something else that can happen. I go to another buyer in another community who doesn't know me. We get to talking and he finds I've driven quite a distance to sell him my furs. He reasons that if he gives me a good price, a price higher than he has been paying his regular customers, I may go back where I came from and spread the word what a great guy so and so is to sell fur to. My chances of this happening are even greater if I have only a small number of furs so that his investment in this advertising campaign will be kept to a minimum.

Yet, when all is said and done, the best way to get the most money for your furs is to deal with a buyer who is concerned about his reputation and who has enough knowledge of the New York market to get the top money for himself and then pass some of the extra income on to you, the trapper. And when a trapper finds such a critter, he would be wise to stay with him.

I've been dealing with the same buyer for the last couple of years and am satisfied that he meets all the requirements. He recognizes me as one of his regular customers and I think that helps. Still, I walk out on him every once in a while. I shop around, keeping my ears open and my nose into the wind.

A curious thing about the individual fur buyer is that he may pay top prices for most furs but pay below everyone else for one particular species. The buyer I deal with always seems a little below everyone else when buying coyote, yet he seems to pay a bit more than the rest for fox.

Next to knowing what furs are selling for, the trapper must sell his furs when prices are highest. In our part of the country, the best time to sell fall-caught furs is just before Christmas. January is another good month. Of course, when the season closes for a particular species, you have little choice but to sell.

I used to think that low prices early in the fall were directly attributable

Figure 16–1 Trappers show their pelts at the Minnesota Trapper's Association fur sale in Grand Rapids, Minnesota. Many received top prices for their furs.

to the poorer quality of early-caught furs. But I've seen none-too-prime pelts bring twice as much late in the season as they did early. I've also seen prices go down. Early one fall a couple of years ago I sold poor-quality muskrat pelts at $5 apiece. Later in the fall, when the pelts began to prime and were obviously of better quality, the price dropped to

Figure 16–2 Checking out a bundle of prime coyote pelts at a fur sale.

$4.25. These fluctuations tend to make the whole business a little confusing, with few guidelines for the novice to count on.

There remains an alternative, and it's a good one. Join your state trapper's association. These organizations usually hold at least one fur sale for its members each year. These sales are a good bet for getting top prices for your furs. I attended a sale held in our state on December 16 in the Armory building in the town of Grand Rapids, Minnesota. Unlike some of the larger state fur sales where an auctioneer is employed and does the selling, this was a more sedate affair.

Trappers were given a number as they entered and assigned a space on the floor to lay out their furs. There were ten buyers (all members of the state trapper's association) and they walked from one collection of furs to another. When a buyer saw something he liked, he made a bid on it. Say you had 12 mink and 9 red fox, nicely handled. The buyer would mark his bid on a piece of paper along with the number assigned to you, and turn it in to one of the several persons in charge. Now another buyer could take a fancy to those same 12 mink and 9 red fox and make a bid on them. In fact, all ten buyers might bid on your furs. At day's end, all that would remain for you to do is to accept the highest bid and pay a token amount toward the rent of the building.

It's a good way to get the best price for your furs and to meet other trappers from around your community and state. Also, it's a good time to find out what other trappers are being offered for their furs, and to see how other trappers handle their furs. I remember one pile of foxes that had not been skinned and looked as though they had been squeezed into a deep freeze. By the looks of their small bodies and ratty tails they were caught well before they were prime. I remember another collection of 25 or so red fox that had been stretched and dried and the furs fairly glowed. I heard later that the poor foxes brought $10 and $15 apiece. The well-handled foxes got up to $110 apiece.

A final word about prices—keep in mind it is the average paid for all your pelts that counts, not just what the buyer is offering for your top furs. When you figure the total number of pelts sold and the total sum paid, the average is often just that—average.

Sources of Supplies

You may find all the supplies you need at a local hunting and sporting goods store. Below are the addresses of suppliers mentioned in the text.

Manufacturers

Allcock Manufacturing Co.
Havahart Box 551
Ossining, NY 10562

Blake and Lamb, Inc.
Cambridge, NY 12816

Raymond Thompson Co.
15815 Second Place West
Lynwood, WN 98036

Woodstream Corp.
Lititz, PA 17543

Suppliers

L. L. Bean, Inc.
Freeport, ME 04033

O. L. Butcher Trapping Supplies
Shushan, NY 12873

Cronk's Outdoor Supplies
Wiscasset, ME 04578

E. J. Dailey's Lures & Baits
P.O. Box 38
Union Hill, NY 14563

S. Stanley Hawbaker & Sons
258 Hawbaker Drive South
Fort Loudon, PA 17224

Northwest Trapper's Supply
Box 408
Owatonna, MN 55060

Northwoods Trapline and Hunting
  Supplies
Box 25
Thief River Falls, MN 56701

Index

Illustrations shown in **boldface**

194

INDEX

INDEX